D0592386

THE ADVERTISING AND
PROMOTION CHALLENGE

WHARTON EXECUTIVE LIBRARY
Yoram J. Wind, Editor
The Wharton School, University of Pennsylvania

F. Gerard Adams
The Business Forecasting Revolution: Nation–Industry–Firm

Leonard M. Lodish
The Advertising and Promotion Challenge:
Vaguely Right or Precisely Wrong?

David Solomons
Making Accounting Policy:
The Quest for Credibility in Financial Reporting

Other titles to be announced.

THE ADVERTISING AND PROMOTION CHALLENGE
Vaguely Right or Precisely Wrong?

Leonard M. Lodish

WITHDRAWN
IOWA STATE UNIVERSITY LIBRARY

New York · Oxford
OXFORD UNIVERSITY PRESS
1986

Oxford University Press

Oxford   New York   Toronto
Delhi   Bombay   Calcutta   Madras   Karachi
Petaling Jaya   Singapore   Hong Kong   Tokyo
Nairobi   Dar es Salaam   Cape Town
Melbourne   Auckland

and associated companies in
Beirut   Berlin   Ibadan   Nicosia

Copyright © 1986 by Oxford University Press, Inc.

Published by Oxford University Press, Inc.,
200 Madison Avenue, New York, New York 10016

Oxford is a registered trademark of Oxford University Press

All rights reserved. No part of this publication may be reproduced,
stored in a retrieval system, or transmitted, in any form or by any means,
electronic, mechanical, photocopying, recording, or otherwise,
without the prior permission of Oxford University Press.

Library of Congress Cataloging-in-Publication Data
Lodish, Leonard M.
The Advertising and promotion challenge
(The Wharton executive library)
Bibliography: p.
Includes index.
1. Advertising.   2. Sales promotion.
I. Title.
HF5821.L58   1986   659.1   85-18864
ISBN 0-19-503702-2

Printing (last digit): 9 8 7 6 5 4 3 2 1

Printed in the United States of America
on acid free paper

To three very important influences on me—John D. C. Little who has been my professional role model since I was his graduate student in 1965; my wife, Susan, who has been my best friend since we were both 13; and my parents, Sylvia and Nathan Lodish, who have been very supportive personal role models.

Series Foreword

The Wharton Executive Library is designed to fill a critical need for a new kind of book for managers. The rapidly changing business environment poses a major challenge to senior executives that cannot be met by the traditional strategies that produced yesterday's and today's winners. Technological advances and their diffusion, dramatic changes in the structure of key industries that result from government deregulation, the rising tide of mergers and acquisitions, the change in consumer lifestyles, and the internationalization of business are some of the forces management must contend with.

Modern business schools are aware of these challenges and much current business research is concerned with finding concepts and methods to help managers solve their new range of problems. However, it can take as long as five years for useful academic work to reach managers—progressing through presentations at academic meetings, limited circulation of working papers, publication of scholarly journals, and finally perhaps reaching publication in one of the nontechnical journals directed at practicing managers. Given the nature of the current business environment, this is too long a delay.

The Wharton Executive Library provides executives with state-of-the-art books in key management areas without the usual time-lag. To enhance their usefulness, each book is:

- Up to date; reflects the latest and best research
- Authoritative; authors are experts in their fields
- Brief; can be read reasonably quickly
- Nontechnical; avoids unnecessary jargon and methodology
- Practical; includes many examples and applications of the concepts discussed
- Compact; can be carried easily in briefcases on business travel

Senior managers will find the volumes in the series to be especially valuable. Because of the books' readability, top management can use them to assess whether their key managers are aware of and using the latest concepts in, for example, marketing, forecasting, financial accounting, finance, strategic planning, information systems, management of technology, human resources, and managing multinational corporations. Given the strong interdependency among the various management functions, it is essential that senior executives be aware of the best academic thinking in the areas for which they are ultimately responsible.

The qualities that make these books useful to managers should make them equally valuable as assigned reading in executive development programs in colleges and universities and management training programs in industry. They can also be used as supplementary reading in academic business courses where their state-of-the-art content should nicely complement theoretical material in standard textbooks.

It is appropriate that this new series should originate in the Wharton School, the first business school founded in the United States—and probably in the world. Its faculty is at the top of its profession, and its graduates fill the management ranks at all levels in all parts of the world. The school's academic focus is on the functional areas of management with an analytic and empirical approach. This quality and approach are clearly evident in these books.

We, the series editor and the publisher, hope that you, the reader, will share our enthusiasm for the series and find the advice of some of the leading scholars in their fields, as presented in these books, of value to you.

We also welcome any suggestions and comments from our readers that will help us to find new and useful titles and achieve the widest possible audience for the books.

YORAM (JERRY) WIND
The Lauder Professor
The Wharton School
University of Pennsylvania
Series Editor

Preface

"If you believe advertising and promotion work, then obviously more advertising or promotion is better than less." A senior executive of a successful consumer goods company recently used this statement to justify increasing advertising and promotion expenditures over the recent past. This executive is wrong and is missing out on many opportunities for increasing the firm's profits by improving advertising and promotion decisions.

In this book we describe other faulty rationales that underlie advertising and promotion decisions. Most of these rationales lead to methods that are very precise and decisions that are very easy to implement. But we will argue that they are "precisely wrong."

We will show in this book that there are much better, but not as precise methods for making advertising and promotion decisions. We term these methods "vaguely right." In order to improve advertising and promotion decisions, changes may be needed in the way marketing departments are organized, the way marketing people are evaluated, the way decisions are made and reviewed, and the way outside vendors are dealt with.

The potential for productivity improvements in advertising and promotions is enormous. In the early part of this century John Wanamaker, a pioneering retailer, was supposed to have said that half of his advertising budget was wasted, but that he didn't know which half. This book describes successful methods and concepts to improve these percentages.

The first part of the book discusses appropriate roles for advertising and promotion and their relationship to broader market and corporate strategy. Next it explores the relationship between roles and operational objectives. Within the appropriate roles and objectives, "vaguely right" approaches needed for copy and budget decisions are described. Alternative ways of obtaining advertising and promotional services are evaluated. The book concludes with the necessary decision support—research, testing, and experiments that are a key element of a vaguely right, more productive approach to improved advertising and promotion.

The challenge of this book is to create a new mode of thinking about advertising and promotion, a mode of thinking that was well stated by the chairman of American Express, who was recently quoted as saying: "A marketing campaign isn't worth doing unless it serves three purposes. It must grow the business, create news and enhance our image."

Many people have influenced the ideas and their communication in this book. Jerry Wind has been an excellent editor, greatly helping with presentation and organization. Lew Pringle of BBDO and Morris Holbrook of Columbia University read the entire manuscript and provided very useful feedback. My Wharton colleagues Erin Anderson, Charles Goodman, David Reibstein, and Barton Weitz were also very insightful reviewers. Irv Gross, an old Wharton colleague, also affected many of these ideas. My colleagues at Management Decision Systems (MDS), now a subsidiary of Information Resources, Inc., all helped to implement many of these ideas in the real world of our clients. In particular, Dinyar Chavda, Jim Findley, Peter Guadagni, Tony Hatoun, Rick Karash, Gerry Katz, Bob Klein, Ken Knipmeyer, John Little, Ellen Shulman, Kerry Simpson, Mike Thoma, Glen Urban, and Jay Wurts were very helpful over the years. Magid Ibrahim and I have together been evaluating promotion programs and developing new methodology at MDS for three years. This interaction has had an important effect on these ideas. Mrs. Berniece Jordan was an excellent word processor through three drafts. Declan Murphy helped to polish my language. Many Wharton students provided very useful comments on early drafts.

I'd like to thank those people who have been my best clients over the years—those who I've learned so much from—Donald Bolster of Horton Church and Goff, Ralph Guild of McGavren Guild Radio, Ralph Leisle, Alan King, and Dean Saddler of J.C. Penney, Darryl Hazel of Ford, Richard Ireland of Valley Forge Investment Corporation, Tom Meyer of Procter and Gamble, Allen Markowitz of Brokers Mortgage Service, Bob Hoffsis and Barbara Connor of Bell of Pennsylvania, Terry Overton of Merck and Company, Joe Kaplan and Ben Ashcom of American Health Systems, and Stanley Federman, and Betsy Wood Knapp at Telmar.

Finally, we live communally with the Spitz Family who have been supportive and tolerant of my work. Besides the steadfast support I get from my wife Susan, my children Max, Jake, and Chaim sacrificed time with me so I could write. I appreciate their sacrifice and hope to make it up to them.

Philadelphia L.M.L.
January 1986

Contents

THE ADVERTISING AND
PROMOTION CHALLENGE

❖ 1 ❖

Overview of Advertising
and Promotion Decisions

The magnitude of expenditures for advertising and promotion in most firms is enormous compared to the attention chief executive officers (CEOs) or senior executives give to them. For example, how many senior managers could answer the following questions about their organizations:

- Do you know the return on investment (R.O.I.) on your investments in advertising or promotion?
- Has the productivity of your advertising and promotion expenditures been increasing or decreasing over time?
- Have you ever tried to measure the productivity of your advertising and promotion expenditures?
- What percentage of your profits is being spent on advertising and promotion?
- What role should the CEO and senior executives take in the management of advertising and promotion?

For many firms, the amount spent on advertising and promotion is a large percentage of their earnings. In 1982, total corporate profits were $417 billion. Of that amount, $65 billion was spent on just media advertising. Thus, advertising accounted for 16% of total profits. The amount spent on promotion is harder to calculate because it encompasses varied expenditures across companies. However, experts estimate that for many firms promotion expenses are at least equal to the amount

3

spent on advertising. Thus, for many firms advertising and promotion expenses amount to at least 32% of corporate profits.

The Learning Curve

Given the magnitude of the problem, it is disappointing to note how little advertisers and promoters have learned about these investments. Over time, the learning curve has not been applicable to advertising and promotion investments. But why?

The learning or experience curve is the graphic representation of the inverse relationship between production costs and production volume: that is, production costs per unit decline as production volume increases. Figure 1-1, a learning curve for production costs, applies to operations and distribution, not advertising and promotion. It is a powerful strategic concept that has had a major impact on management thought. The learning curve has impelled many companies to undertake strategic initiatives designed to increase market share and, thus, take advantage of the economies that derive from the cumulative experience of producing the same product many times over. For many products, especially in electronics and other high technology areas, manufacturing costs per unit of output are decreasing significantly. Other areas of company operations have also been subject to learning curve effects. For example, distribution costs have declined significantly as new technologies for the transport of goods—such as containerization and computer-aided routing—developed.

There are some business activities, however, that have not benefited from learning curve effects. For example, most marketing costs per unit have generally not declined as products have become larger and larger sellers. Consequently, most CEOs and senior executives are still uncertain about the productivity of the money they are spending on advertising and promotion. As one CEO said over 50 years ago, "I know that 50% of my advertising budget is being wasted. But I don't know which half."

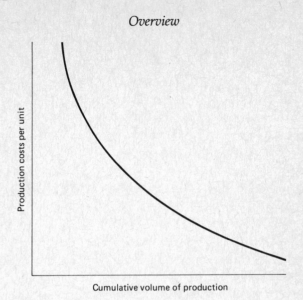

Figure 1-1. The learning curve for operations and distribution production costs.

Most chief executive officers would agree with this statement. In a 1980 survey of CEOs by Professor F. E. Webster of Dartmouth, CEOs mentioned concern about marketing productivity second only to concerns about lack of marketing innovation. The percentage of return (i.e., in the form of improved productivity in advertising and promotion) for each corporate dollar spent has not kept pace with either the improvement or the return found in other areas of use of corporate resources. If productivity progress in the rest of a firm's resources were as slow as it is in advertising and promotion, the total productivity growth problem in the United States would be much worse than it is.

Measuring Advertising and Promotion Productivity

When applied to advertising and promotion, the usual definition of productivity creates severe measurement problems. Productivity is customarily defined as units of output divided by units of input. Typically, the output is goods and services and the input is factors of production. In advertising and promotion, the primary input (i.e., money) is measurable. However, the output of advertising and promotion is neither easy to measure nor directly assignable to the advertising and promotion expenses. Advertising and promotion are usually elements of a marketing mix that also includes a product, its price, its packaging, its sales force, its distribution strategy, and its positioning. Isolating the effects of advertising or promotion from the other elements of the marketing mix is a difficult task. Not only can a particular company's own marketing mix affect the productivity of its advertising and promotion, but the competition's marketing mix, the dynamics of the ultimate consumer, and outside environmental forces are constantly changing. These factors do not make measurement easy.

To complicate matters even more, some advertising is not related to sales of a particular product, but has a loftier mission. Examples include advocacy advertising, corporate image advertising, or advertising to the financial community. How is the output of that kind of advertising measured? If progress in productivity of advertising or promotion cannot be measured, then how can the learning curve contribute to improved productivity in investments in advertising and promotion?

In most cases, executives have ignored the problem of measuring the productivity of advertising. Instead, management concentrates on the measurable aspects of advertising and promotion such as awareness, recall, or costs. However, as the rest of this book will show, most of those precisely measured outputs are not related to the legitimate strategic and tactical objectives of advertising and promotion. It is human nature to focus on that which can be measured precisely and to ignore that which is difficult to measure. The author's conclusion about advertising and promotion is the same one reached earlier in studying sales force management problems.[1]

Vaguely Right Rather than Precisely Wrong
Decision Making

It is preferable for executives to be "vaguely right" rather than "precisely wrong" in their evaluation of advertising and promotion alternatives. This vaguely right-precisely wrong concept was first introduced by Sidney Davidson in 1970 in *Forbes* Magazine. He applied it to evaluating accounting statements to determine the investment value of a company. According to Davidson, most of the real assets and liabilities of companies are not precisely measured by any income statement or balance sheet. Instead, a company's worth is determined by "imprecise" measures such as the strength of their management, their growth prospects, and the company's reputation. Such measures are more important to evaluating the company's continuing worth than the value of buildings purchased 25 years ago.[2]

This concept also applies to advertising and promotion strategy. Just as bad money drives out good money, hard (precisely wrong) data seems to drive out soft (vaguely right) data in advertising and promotion decisions.

What does this have to do with the chief executive officer's running of the division or company? The CEO can change the low level of progress seen in advertising and promotion productivity by changing the way the firm evaluates advertising and promotion decisions. In other words, senior management must begin to insist on vaguely right rather than precisely wrong answers to routine strategic and tactical advertising and promotion questions.

The basic message of this book is that there are much better (i.e., vaguely right) methods for making and evaluating advertising and promotion decisions. However, the way advertising and promotion departments are organized, the way outside vendors are dealt with, the way decisions are made, and the way the people involved with those decisions are evaluated, may all contribute to promoting precisely wrong approaches to advertising and promotion decisions. Senior executives can change organization, procedures for dealing with vendors, procedures for making decisions, and the way managers are evaluated. But the problem is too important to be completely delegated to middle management.

As shown in subsequent chapters, the problem of measuring advertising and promotional effectiveness is not susceptible to short-term, "quick fix," solutions. Measuring the effectiveness of advertising and promotion requires developing long-term programs that gradually improve estimates of their real effectiveness. Unfortunately, such long-term programs involve continual short-term costs, for example, experimentation and research, lost product sales, and administration. Most of these short-term costs are precisely measurable. However, it takes time to obtain the long-term benefits that are not precisely measurable. If managers are evaluated only on their short-term success or failure on precisely measurable variables, then a long-term advertising and promotion productivity improvement program will never succeed.

There is hope, however. Anheuser Busch is one firm that has instituted a testing and experimentation program to get some of the vaguely right answers. These programs, which were put in place over 5 to 10 years, had significant impact on the performance of the firm. Ackoff and Emshoff document how these long-term programs helped the firm to increase sales and profits while simultaneously decreasing their advertising costs per barrel.[3]

Senior executives should insist that the performance objectives of all marketing managers involved with advertising and promotion should include improving the long-term productivity of advertising and promotion decisions. Some decisions should be justified on how they will improve future sales and profits rather than on the consequences of current sales and profits. Some of the most important decisions of this type include those that involve choosing programs for measuring the actual (i.e., vaguely right) impact of advertising and promotion.

In most firms, marketing managers have no incentive to take actions that would improve the long-term measurement of advertising and promotion productivity. They are only judged on the short-term sales (and sometimes profit) implications of their actions. Thus, since measurement of advertising and promotion productivity is typically associated with increasing costs or decreasing sales during the short term, most marketing managers are not judged on the long-term help they bring the company.

How many management by objective (MBO) programs include measurement of advertising and promotion productivity? The following chapters will show that it is in senior management's best interest to develop motivational programs to reward managers for improving their measurements of advertising and promotion productivity.

Avoiding Precisely Wrong Decision Making

Subsequent chapters of this book will investigate various types of precisely wrong decisions and compare them to vaguely right procedures. For example, more marketing managers are concerned with precisely measurable product sales than with product profits. Product profits are much harder to estimate because of the various cost allocations that must be made. When evaluating performance of an advertising budget, most managers consider media reach, frequency, awareness, and recall (all of which can be measured with reasonable precision by consumer surveys), or available syndicated data. However, these advertising sub-goals are not necessarily related to changes in consumer behavior. A media buy is said to be a good media buy if it obtains lots of gross rating points per dollar. A gross rating point is a measure of advertising exposures to a demographically defined audience. However, how many firms are able to evaluate these per dollar changes in consumer behavior? If consumers do not change either long-term or short-term purchasing behavior as the result of an advertising or promotional

Table 1-1. Some Decision Alternatives

Problem Area	Precisely Wrong Criteria	Vaguely Right Criteria
Product/Market Management	Short-term sales	Long-term profits
Advertising Budget	Reach and frequency Product awareness Advertising recall	Changes in buyer behavior—long-term or short-term—and its resulting profitability
Media Planning	Gross rating points per dollar Reach and frequency	Changes in buyer behavior per dollar
Promotion Management	Promotion costs	Changes in buyer behavior and resulting long- and short-term profits
Trade Promotion Management	Amount sold to the trade on deal Amount sold to the trade compared to the trade's normal purchases	Change in buyer behavior of the ultimate consumer
Consumer Coupons	Redemption rates and costs	Sales and profit changes (both short- and long-term) caused by the coupons

program, then the program has no value. But how many companies are measuring such program-related changes in consumer behavior? Most firms evaluate the cost of promotion, but few firms even attempt to measure the profitability of a long- or short-term promotion compared to not doing the promotion at all.

Table 1-1 shows some examples of precisely wrong criteria commonly used for evaluating promotions to both trade intermediaries and the ultimate consumer. In general, many executives concentrate too much on the costs and the precisely measurable outcomes of advertising and promotion and too little on measuring the real benefits.

Senior Management's Role in Making Vaguely Right Decisions

These precisely wrong procedures and measurements are deeply ingrained into the marketing decision making structures of most consumer, industrial, and service firms. Change will not be forthcoming, however, unless senior management takes a firm stand against these procedures and promotes decisions that rationally consider both long-term and short-term effects. If senior managers do not take this posture, advertising and promotion expenditures—which may be a significant portion of the firm's resource allocation—will continue to be justified as they always have. Senior management cannot shy away. They must know enough to ask the right questions and poke through the jargon that accompanies the precisely wrong criteria. In fact, the main purpose of this book is to provide senior executives with enough information so that they can begin to penetrate the jargon and ask the right questions. Eventually, if the firm develops and implements a more rational pattern of advertising and promotion decision making, senior management may not have to pay as much attention to advertising and promotion decisions. In order to really turn the company's decision-making procedures around, significant changes must be made in the way advertising and promotion decisions are reached. Typical senior executives should be paying much more attention to this decision-making process than they are now.

Aside from the increases in productivity that can result from more senior management attention to advertising and promotion, there are other compelling reasons for them to become involved. Corporate advertising is the most visible sign of the way the firm wants to be perceived. Thus, corporate advertising must be consistent and supportive of the vision the CEO has for the firm. Forging a common vision is one of the most important, if not the most important, job of a CEO. The now classic Avis "We Try Harder" campaign had as much of an affect on Avis employees and suppliers as it did on the car renting market.

Only the CEO or a delegate can make sure that advertising

and promotion for each of the firm divisions or strategic business units (SBU's) is consistent with the corporate mission and value system. All the divisions of General Motors (GM), for example, should portray a consistent picture to the corporate stakeholders of who and what GM is and stands for. Each stakeholder—such as the car buyer, auto dealers, competitors, and the U.S. and foreign governments—may see or hear GM advertising and develop perceptions from it. In other words, what Cadillac says about "Body by Fisher" should be consistent with what Chevrolet says.

Plan of the Book

Given the pragmatic objectives of this book, no attempt is made to provide a complete treatment of advertising and promotion. Concentration is on those areas in which senior management can have a positive influence on improving the quality of decisions. I also provide enough conceptual material so that the executive can ask reasonable questions. This material is general enough to be useful to executives in all industries including industrial and consumer products and services.

Before summarizing the book's plan for achieving these objectives, the subject should be defined. Philip Kotler defines advertising as "nonpersonal forms of communication conducted through paid media under clear sponsorship." He defines promotions as "tools of a short term incentive nature, designed to stimulate earlier and/or stronger target market response." Included as promotion tools are "coupons, premiums, and contests for consumer markets, buying allowances, cooperative advertising allowances, and free goods for distributors and dealers; discounts, gifts, and extras for industrial users, and sales contests and special bonuses for members of the sales force."[4]

This book purposely covers advertising and promotion decisions together. Both functions are integral, interrelated elements of the marketing mix. Advertising and promotion may be synergistic or cannibalistic, depending on how they are planned and executed, for example:

1. In many firms the same people are affecting decisions in both areas.
2. Both areas have much difficulty in productivity measurement.
3. Many concepts are appropriate for managing both functions.
4. Both areas have budget, copy, and media decisions.
5. Both areas have similar problems in decision support systems.
6. Both areas involve dealing with outside vendors.
7. Both areas have long- and short-term consequences needing consideration.

The book continues with Chapters 2 and 3 discussing appropriate roles for advertising and promotion. Since appropriate roles must be an outgrowth of corporate and marketing strategy, Chapter 4 examines the relationship between advertising and promotion and the marketing mix, marketing strategy, and corporate strategy. Chapter 5 discusses the interrelated task of determining advertising and promotion objectives. The next three chapters discuss rational approaches to the tactical decisions required for advertising and promotion progress. Chapter 6 examines budget decisions, Chapter 7 discusses copy (what to say), and Chapter 8 explores media (where to say it). Each chapter describes ways in which senior management can influence the tactical decision process so as to improve its productivity. Chapter 9 develops alternative structures for obtaining effective advertising and promotion services and methods of implementing the structures in terms of evaluating alternative suppliers. It also reviews (1) when to change suppliers and (2) the motivation and compensation of suppliers. Chapter 10 provides an overview of the costs and benefits of methods for supporting advertising and promotion decisions. The crucial influence of the CEO and senior management on the process for evaluation of research and information relating to advertising and promotion is underscored. Finally, Chapter 11 sets forth some summary questions.

Table 1-2 summarizes the important questions covered in each chapter.

Table 1-2.   Basic Questions Covered in Each Chapter

Chapter 2—How To Use Advertising

- What are appropriate roles for advertising?
- How is advertising related to product positioning and market segmentation?
- What are roles for advertising other than in selling products or services, such as corporate advertising?

Chapter 3—Promotion: A Tool in Market Positioning?

- What are the appropriate roles for promotion?
- How is promotion related to product positioning and market segmentation?
- What are roles for both advertising and promotion for new product introduction?

Chapter 4—Advertising and Promotion/Marketing Mix/Marketing Strategy

- How is the marketing mix related to marketing strategy?
- How are advertising and promotion related to the marketing mix and to marketing strategy?

Chapter 5—Setting the Objectives

- How should roles be translated into objectives?
- How should objectives be related to long-term sales and profits?
- How should management develop operational objectives for advertising and promotion?

Chapter 6—Advertising and Promotion Budgeting

- What are some "precisely wrong" rules of thumb for budgeting advertising and promotion expenditures?
- How is testing related to budgeting?
- How should long term vs. short term trade-offs be made?
- How are budgets related to media, copy, and other elements of the marketing mix?

Chapter 7—Copy Decisions

- How should the creative activity be structured, managed, and evaluated?
- How is this creative process related to testing methods?
- How important is copy?
- How can management improve the validity and reliability of copy test?

Chapter 8—Media Decisions

- Who really cares and who should care about media decisions?
- What are "precisely wrong" rules of thumb for evaluating media plans?
- What are "vaguely right" approaches for media plan development?
- What is the role of media research and experimentation?

- What are the advantages and disadvantages of alternative methods for obtaining advertising and promotion services?
- What are the strengths and weaknesses of alternative compensation methods for outside services?
- When should suppliers be changed? How should new suppliers be evaluated?

- What is the difference to management between market status and market response reporting?
- What are elements needed for effective decision support?
- How should managers relate to a decision support system?
- How does testing relate to decision support?

- What can top managers do to be "vaguely right"?
- What can marketing managers do to be "vaguely right"?

We hope that by the time senior managers have read these chapters, they have a better appreciation of the role they can play in improving the productivity of the firm's advertising and promotion decisions.

Summary and Action Questions

- How is the effectiveness of the company's advertising programs being measured?
- Are current programs designed for long- or short-term benefits? How do these benefits support the company's marketing objectives and overall strategic plans?
- What type of incentives could be employed to better the company's advertising or promotion productivity? Design a list of incentives that would benefit the long-term measurement of both advertising and promotion.
- Make a list of some possible long- and short-term advertising benefits. How many of these can be directly related to the company in its present position?
- What is the real benefit of advertising? How could the firm use it more effectively to improve profitability?

Further Reading

D. A. Aaker and J. M. Carmon, "Are You Over Advertising," *Journal of Marketing* (August 1982), pp. 56–69. An excellent article summarizing empirical evidence and some hypotheses as to why some advertising expenditures may not be productive.

L. M. Lodish, "A Marketing Decision Support System for Retailers," *Marketing Science* (Winter 1982), pp. 31–56. An overview of how a large chain retailer has implemented a rational approach to advertising and promotion decisions.

Donald C. Marschner, "DAGMAR Revisited—Eight Years Later," *Journal of Advertising Research*, 2:29 (April 1971). This reference describes one method of generating advertising objectives and evaluating advertising.

Alfred G. Oxenfeldt and Carroll Swan, *Management of the Advertising Function* (New York: Wadsworth Publishing Co., In., 1961). A summary of standard methods for evaluating advertising that have not changed in practice very much.

Notes

1. Leonard M. Lodish, "A Vaguely Right Approach to Sales Force Allocations," *Harvard Business Review* (January–February 1974), pp. 119–125.
2. Sidney Davidson, "As I See It," *Forbes* (April 1, 1970), p. 40.
3. R. A. Ackoff, and J. R. Emshoff, "Advertising Research at Anheuser Busch, Inc. (1963–68)," *Sloan Management Review* (Winter and Spring 1975).
4. Philip Kotler, *Marketing Management*, 4th Edition (Englewood Cliffs, N.J.: Prentice-Hall, 1980), pp. 497, 526.

❖ 2 ❖

How To Use Advertising

In order to manage the advertising function effectively, one of the critical issues that must be addressed quite early in the decision-making process is the appropriate role of advertising. But what are these roles? The chief executive officer (CEO) and senior management must be able to answer the following questions to get the answer:

- What are appropriate roles for advertising?
- How is advertising related to product positioning and market segmentation?
- How are advertising roles related to management control of advertising and promotion?
- What are other roles for advertising besides selling products or services?
- How does trade advertising relate to the roles of advertising?

This chapter will discuss the appropriate roles for advertising in both marketing and corporate strategy. Chapter 3 will similarly examine some appropriate roles for promotion. However, the appropriate roles for advertising and promotion are not assigned in a vacuum. They must be considered an outgrowth of corporate and marketing strategy. If the role of advertising is inconsistent with corporate and marketing strategies, then the advertising may be counterproductive. The latter aspect will be examined in Chapter 4.

Consistent with the discussion in Chapter 1, a basic criterion of effective advertising is that either the long- or short-run profitability of the firm is higher than it would have been in the absence of such advertising. This profitability criterion, however, is not sufficient to validate the advertising. There are constraints under which firms must operate. For example, advertising that substantially deceives the population should not be undertaken.

Do not assume that the list of appropriate roles for advertising discussed below is all inclusive. New creative roles for advertising are found every day. This chapter first discusses the need for roles and characterizes the general advertising role types. It then examines the more standard advertising roles, shows how they can be improved by integration with positioning concepts, and then examines some recently emerged creative new roles.

Advertising Roles

An explicit statement in the marketing plan about the appropriate roles for advertising and promotion has many benefits for the firm. The most important benefit is that the specific roles that the advertising or promotion is to fill can then be translated into objectives for the advertising and promotion to achieve.

Measurable, operational goals put the executive back in contol of the decision making for, and implementation of, advertising and promotion. Simply stating that advertising and promotion should raise sales and profits is not enough. It is much more effective to determine the functions or the roles that the advertising and promotion must perform.

As we will see in this chapter's discussion of the roles of advertising, there are a number of interlocking roles that advertising can perform. Basically, these roles can be categorized in three groups: (1) The function of the first group of roles is increasing the number of customers or increasing the rate of use of the product or service by current customers; (2) the second grouping of roles postulates the perceptual changes that advertising is supposed to affect; (3) the third role grouping concentrates on creating advertising that will by itself cause people to do

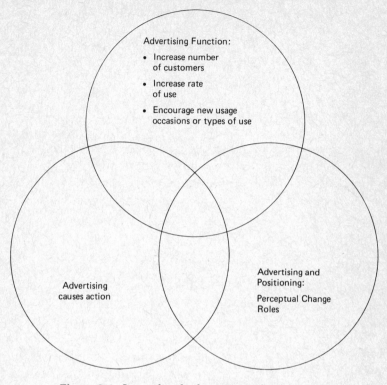

Figure 2-1. Interrelated advertising roles from the
advertiser's perspective.

something. It's one thing for perceptions to change, it's another for people to actually pick up the phone or take a walk and order something. In many cases, this role is sufficient in itself to judge the success of advertising. For example, department store or direct response advertising can be judged directly by its action in terms of orders or leads that may be generated.

Figure 2-1 shows how these three types of roles may be considered simultaneously while setting objectives for an advertising campaign. One can combine roles of product positioning that may be needed to induce increasing numbers of people to use a particular product and to precipitate action. Recently, the Campbell Soup Company changed its strategy to increase the number of people using soup. They expect their advertising campaign to gain their normal 80% market share of the new users. The campaign intends to convince people that soup is a nourishing food. Therefore, the perceptual role of the advertising is to increase people's perception of soup as a nutritionally effective food. Finally, if the campaign is effective and people's perceptions are changed, they will—ideally—go out and buy more soup.

Please note that Figure 2-1 is from the advertiser's perspective. A social critic or consumer group might want to consider advertising's role in shaping the moral or materialistic values of our society. These other "stakeholders" provide constraints on the kind of roles that are feasible for firms to utilize.

Role Group 1: Customers and Their Product Use

For most marketers, normal product advertising plays two basic roles. First, it increases, or should increase, the number of customers for a brand. Second, it increases or should increase, the rate of use among current customers for the brand. These roles are appropriate for a very broad definition of "product" and "customer." The same roles that Procter & Gamble would consider using for a frequently purchased household consumer product might also be appropriate for a product such as industrial data processing equipment, or getting people to use seat belts or getting people to stop smoking. These two basic roles, increasing the number of customers and increasing the rate of use, can be subdivided into more specific parts that advertising might play.

Increasing the number of customers can be done in at least three ways: First, we can get customers who had been buying our competitor's product to begin buying ours, that is, market share can be increased at the expense of our competition. Second, current buyers can be deterred from switching to our

competition, that is, we can retain more loyalty among our current customers. Finally, the total market for the product class
as a whole can be expanded by attracting new customers to the
category. We can increase the *rate of use* for those who are already using our product by either getting them to use more, or
by finding new uses for the product.

Some classic advertising successes can be related to the appropriate choice of roles for the advertising to play. The advertising of Arm & Hammer baking soda as a deodorant for refrig-
erators is a good example of (1) expanding the total market for
the product class by showing people a new use and (2) getting
increasing usage from current customers by also showing them
the new use. The "Pepsi Challenge" campaign has the dual role
of converting customers from other colas to Pepsi and causing
Pepsi buyers to continue to buy Pepsi by reinforcing the perception that Pepsi tastes better than Coke.

These standard advertising roles are not as precise as they
could be for guiding advertising decision making. A key reason
for their imprecision is that there is no reason given for *how* the
advertising is to increase either the number of customers or the
rate of use among current customers. More specific and effective roles for advertising can be delineated when advertising is
considered as a part of the product positioning decision.

Product Positioning

Positioning decisions take the viewpoint of the customer. Because they get at the why of the workings of advertising, positioning concepts have proven helpful in determining appropriate roles for advertising. Positioning is defined as "a
managerial activity in which management tries to deliver a perceived offering that is preferred by a significant segment of the
market and therefore bought."

The concepts of perception and preference in the above definition are important for developing productive advertising.
Perception addresses how the customer views both the com-

pany's offering and those of any competitors. These perceptions may involve a product's personality, its attributes, or its
image. Preference refers to those combinations of personality,
attributes, or image the customer favors in making the trade-
off on which products to purchase or to use.

Advertising can affect positioning in two fundamental ways:
it can change either perceptions or preferences. Most advertising attempts to change or reinforce existing perceptions of
products vis-à-vis the competition. Miller Brewing Company
successfully used advertising to change the public's perception
of Miller beer. What had been a beer for women became a beer
for the working man. The advertising employed completely
changed the personality and image of the product. Miller also
succeeded in changing the perception of dietetic (i.e., "lite") beer
from a "sissy" product to a "he-man" product by using ath-
letes and macho people as spokesmen. The success of both Miller
and Miller Lite has been exceptional. Executives with very good
marketing skills and creativity decided on appropriate roles for
advertising for both products.

Role Group 2: Perceptions and Preferences

Standard market research techniques are currently available
to measure consumer product perceptions on the attributes or
dimensions that they use to differentiate products. However,
to decide how advertising should change perceptions in a specific case, the marketer must know which aspects of perceptions are important to various groups of people. The marketer
needs answers to these questions:

- How important is each perceived attribute compared to other
  attributes?
- How is the competition perceived?
- What is feasible?

Thus, not only should market research reveal current consumer perceptions, it should also relate perceptions to consumer choice via consumer preferences. That is, how do con-

sumers trade-off perceived attributes of a product in making their purchase decisions?

There are a number of satisfactory market research techniques that can estimate the trade-offs that consumers are making when they buy goods and services. Once these trade-offs have been developed and a model of the competitive consumer choice process is obtained, the marketer can then ask questions about the sales and share effects of changing the product's perception: "If I can make consumers perceive my laundry detergent as equally effective on whites as product A, and as equally gentle as product B, I would then increase my market share over the long run from 10% to about 14%." However, if the product is not perceived to deliver what the advertising portrays, the advertising will usually be counterproductive. This is particularly true when a product is dependent on repeat purchase to become profitable. Overselling the product, by promising attributes that the consumer does not perceive upon use, will cause significant problems when the consumer decides to repurchase.

However, if advertising can correct a legitimate misperception on an important dimension, then the advertising can be extremely productive. At first glance, one would not think that advertising could be a potent force for an industrial fibre drum firm. An *Advertising Age* article recounted the case of Continental Fibre Drum Company, of Stamford, Connecticut.[1] Philip White took over as general manager of sales and marketing in 1974. He commissioned a positioning study of fibre drums versus other forms of packaging to find out why fibre drums were losing out to other forms of packaging. According to Mr. White, "One of the biggest misconceptions was that the drums were okay unless they got wet. They also believed the drums couldn't carry liquids."

A series of print ads, directed toward target company executives at every level, were initiated to combat the misconception. The ad budget was increased from $50,000 to $500,000 to accomplish the new education. One new ad pictured an elephant standing on two drums to show strength. Another ad showed the drums standing in the Okefenokee Swamp to demonstrate they could stand humidity. This campaign not only increased sales, it created new markets.

Changing preferences is the other means by which advertisnig may affect consumer behavior. In this case, advertising attempts to change the trade-offs that consumers make when they purchase. Instead of trying to say that the particular product is different, the advertising tries to convince consumers that they should change their decisions to reflect their preference for the product's attributes. For example, an American car manufacturer might attempt to convince a segment of the buying public that buying American cars is their patriotic duty. Thus, they should weight the attribute "made in the U.S.A." a lot more when they buy cars. This advertising does not attempt to change the perception of American cars. Instead, it focuses on convincing the consumer that buying an American-made product should be a very important factor in their decision making.

The differences between these two roles of advertising vis-à-vis product positioning relate to the marketing concept. The first role, changing perceptions, is to convince people that a particular product or service satisfies their needs. The second role, trying to change preferences, is to convince people to change their needs to accommodate our particular product. In general, it is much easier to change perceptions than it is to change preferences.

Some of the most effective marketing programs utilize both roles, simultaneously changing perception and preference. Typically, this is accomplished by finding a new attribute or dimension to use to differentiate a product that no other firm in the product category has used before. Quaker's 100% Natural Granola cereal is an example of creating a new dimension. Before Quaker, no one had described cereals as natural in the mass market. Quaker simultaneously positioned their product as good on the natural attribute and convinced some people that natural was something that was important in buying cereal. Similarly, Vick's Nyquil, when it was first introduced, was unique from all the other cold remedies because it was positioned as a nighttime remedy. Vick's created the attribute nighttime versus daytime and convinced some people that a special nighttime remedy was more to their liking since that's the way they used a number of cold products.

Category and Selling Positioning

F. B. Ennis took a different, complementary approach to classifying positioning roles.[2] He divided positioning concepts into groups: category positioning and selling positioning. Category positioning refers to the market, product category, or market segment in which the brand wishes to compete.

> Consider the case of Lever's Wisk liquid detergent and the marketing advantages it enjoys today by just such positioning. Wisk is a heavy-duty liquid detergent similar to Procter & Gamble's Era and Colgate's Dynamo. Though it actively competes with them, it is perhaps more competitive to S.C. Johnson & Son's Shout spot remover because Wisk has been positioned as the best brand for eliminating tough stains, such as "rings around the collar." The result has been a generally steady market share for Wisk while Era and Dynamo battle for share points.

The second classification, selling positioning, refers to how the potential consumer is to perceive the product in order to differentiate it from its competitors. Ennis makes a distinction between those products that use positioning based on actual product characteristics and those that are based on a unique manner in which the consumer is to perceive the product, regardless of its functional attributes. He does not think that easily duplicated functional attributes or attributes that are marginal in terms of preference are very productive as strategic positioning options.

> Look how quickly Pillsbury's pudding cake mixes were matched by the Betty Crocker and Duncan Hines brands, or the speed with

which Lipton's Cup-a-Soup was followed by Nestle's Souptime. Gainesburger with egg out of General Foods was followed in only months by Ken-L Ration Burgers with egg out of Quaker Oats. Schick Super II followed Gillette's Trac II in about eight months.

The marketing of brands in this situation usually deteriorates into a slug fest between opposing field sales forces, coupled with ever increasing allowances to the trade to buy their merchandising co-operation—often at the sacrifice of the brand's consumer franchise.

Ennis believes that product perceptions based on life style or image relevant to the consumer can be much harder to duplicate. For example, the Marlboro man and Miller Lite are successful uses of this type of positioning. Lots of beers can functionally duplicate Miller Lite, but it will be difficult to duplicate its image. Relating a functional product attribute to the needs of the consumer in a unique way is typically a productive strategy. Just describing the product attribute isn't enough. Ennis describes American Optical's successful use of this type of positioning:

An example of this is the approach the American Optical Co. took in the sale of the bifocal eye glasses in which the bifocal line in the glass is eliminated. This was a major new product attribute to middle-aged women who seek to avoid the stigma of aging which is associated with bifocals. Most marketing managers would choose unswervingly to promote this key point of difference as the primary thrust of their selling concept to the public. American Optical took the more sophisticated approach, however, of using a consumer-oriented, sex appeal, positioning concept, i.e., that these glasses will make the wearer look younger and more attractive, relegating the physical innovation of the product to a supporting role for this primary claim.

It is generally more difficult, however, to successfully position a product without meaningful consumer benefits. Successful image products such as Marlboro and Miller Lite don't happen very often in most other product or service categories. For example, James Peil, former Vice President of New Ventures and

Strategic Planning at Miles Laboratories, studied 113 proprietary drug brands in 22 categories.[3] In 12 of the categories, the one time leader had been replaced by another brand. Peil's conclusions about the role of advertising are quite provocative and probably representative of other products and services.

> Leading brands enjoy their position because of overwhelming competitive dominance on one or more product attributes considered vital to consumers. . . . Leaders are fast to defend their positions when competition threatens. Being unprepared to meet product challenges caused the loss of leadership in the 12 cases studied.

> Winning products offer the consumer significant advantages vs. other products on the market. These advantages are real. They come from the product itself or clinical research about the product.

> The role of marketing in these success stories also was important but less important than the product itself.

According to Peil, a familiar pattern emerged among the product failures. Advertising was used to create the illusion of a benefit that didn't exist. The advertising-to-sales ratio for winners consistently was lower than for their competitors.

Positioning Industrial and Service Products

All these advertising and positioning concepts are not applicable solely to frequently purchased consumer products. They are also appropriate for other products and services. For example, Sperry Rand's corporate advertising campaign portrays Sperry as a company that listens better. This campaign is a two-pronged attempt to introduce a new dimension into the way Sperry competes with its rivals. First, the perceived attribute "listening better," is intended to convince people that Sperry's people will perform better than their competitors. Second, it is more advantageous to deal with companies that listen better.

The first proposition involves changing perceptions, the second changing preferences.

Advertising for new products or services has the objective of establishing perceptions for the first time. This advertising is very important and its effectiveness is relatively easy to measure. In most cases, consumers who are not aware of a product and have developed no perceptions of its attributes are not going to buy it. This is true for industrial products as well as consumer products.

Very precise roles for advertising can be defined by integrating product positioning concepts and the more standard advertising functions. Appropriate roles for advertising might include, for example, increasing the rate of use of a product by changing customers' perceptions of the appropriateness of a product for the new use. The Florida orange growers are trying to accomplish this by advertising that it is appropriate to drink orange juice all day long, not just at breakfast. It is not enough to say that one is attempting to convert customers from competing brands. However, it is helpful to say that customers will be converted from competing brands because your product is better than the competing brands on either functional or image attributes that consumers view as important.

Role Group 3: Market Segmentation, Advertising, and Product Positioning

Not all consumers use the same trade-offs in choosing products or services from among competitive offerings. Some marketers have realized that niche strategies concentrating on groups of consumers having similar preferences (that is, similar trade-offs) can be very effective. By homing in on market segments having similar preferences, the provider of the product can develop distinctive differentiation from competitors and develop long-term franchises that may be difficult for competitors to attack. Maytag has developed an excellent consumer franchise by concentrating on that portion of the market that values durability and extremely high quality more than relative price in the selection of washing machines and dishwashers. Not everyone will make the trade-off to buy a Maytag, but there is a significant market segment there that enables Maytag to be consistently more profitable than other competitors in the washing arena.

Similarly, Tylenol has developed a strong consumer franchise for those who are concerned about aspirin side effects as an important attribute of analgesics. Because their long-term strategy sought to convince both doctors and their patients that Tylenol didn't have the same side effects as aspirin, Tylenol was in a good position to retain the majority of the market segment when well-financed competitors tried to muscle in. Even when the terrible event of seven people dying from poisoning of Tylenol capsules hit the brand in 1982, the company was able to substantially recover its prior share. Once the product was repackaged, consumers were evidently able to separate the product's perception from the acts of deranged people. There are also standard market research techniques available to develop market segmentation schemes for positioning most products and services. These market research techniques group and identify people who have similar preferences—that is, people who make similar trade-offs in their purchasing decisions.

Other Advertising Situations

Other specialized advertising roles can be important in supporting marketing strategies. For example, trade or intermediary advertising can be a big leverage point for some marketing strategies. Just as consumers have perceptions and preferences that they use to determine products and services that they buy, intermediaries in the marketing system have perceptions and preferences of products and suppliers that they use to determine whose products they carry, whose products they push, and whose products they do not carry. Strategic questions must be answered before a trade advertising campaign can be launched. These questions include "How does the firm want to be perceived compared to the competition?" and "On which market segments within the trade are they concentrating?"

The same positioning roles of advertising are also conceptually appropriate for trade advertising. The only difference is that the attributes of greatest concern to the trade may be different and their weighting schemes may be different. For example, the perceptual attributes that intermediaries use may involve margin and discounts, speed of delivery, lack of hassle, service, prompt attention to problems, and so forth. If a firm has done something to improve its performance on any one of these attributes, trade advertising may be an effective way to change the perceptions of the intermediaries. Trade advertising may also be useful for changing the perception of particular products. A marketer may want to tell the trade how successful the product has been in other avenues of distribution or how much consumer advertising or promotion is behind the product. These activities may change the trade's image of the product as a candidate for inclusion in their product mix.

Advertising to the trade can also make the salesperson's job easier because some ideas are more easily communicated through advertising than by a salesperson. Especially if a company is trying to open up a new class of trade, the salesperson may find it easier to get in to see the decision makers if proper advertising has been disseminated to the trade.

Corporate Advertising

Positioning concepts are also critical for determining appropriate roles for corporate advertising. Certain questions have to be answered in order to develop a productive corporate advertising campaign, for example: Who are we? What business are we in? How do we want the relevant stakeholders in our business to perceive us? What is important to our stakeholders? Corporate campaigns can perform many useful roles. In many cases, a corporation's products or services are more attractive to potential users or intermediaries because of the reputation of the company that provides the products. IBM and DuPont have used corporate advertising campaigns that for years supported corporate marketing strategies of reinforcing perceptions of their dedication to service and high quality. It is well known among computer professionals that IBM does not always have the most technologically advanced computers, but IBM has a reputation for always solving its customer's problems. This reputation has been enhanced by the corporate image advertising that IBM has undertaken over the years.

When Procter & Gamble introduces a new product, it is typically introduced in advertising as another new product from Procter & Gamble. Procter & Gamble has developed a reputation for quality among many consumers. It is interesting that Procter & Gamble does not emphasize the corporate name after a product has become established because each brand is said to be competing with other Procter & Gamble brands for the consumer's attention. However, Procter & Gamble's reputation does indeed give the products a good start. Having strong corporate identity—that is, a good perception among target markets—can make it much easier to introduce new products, particularly those involving some risk for the consumer.

In some cases, a corporate image may not be appropriate for a particular product. How many people know that G. H. Bass, the maker of preppy Bass Weejun shoes, is owned by Cheeseborough Ponds? The name Cheeseborough Ponds attached to Bass Weejuns and emphasized in advertising would negate the preppy image of Bass as being old and exclusive. Similarly, if people knew that Izod Alligator sportswear was distributed exclusively in the United States by a division of General Mills, Izod's status and image perception would be confused.

The inhabitants of Wall Street or other financial centers may be suitable targets for corporate advertising, *if* there is something to advertise. Stock analysts, brokers, and portfolio managers are all human beings who make decisions based on their perceptions of alternatives. The positioning concepts discussed earlier are appropriate for influencing the decisions of security purchasers. These people recommend stocks whose perceptions are best on dimensions or attributes they consider important. Corporate advertising can be effective in correcting misperceptions that can occur among the financial community. According to Walter P. Margulies:[4]

> More than one CEO has been startled to learn of the misperceptions that prevail on Wall Street. Special steps may be necessary to adjust these perceptions of analysts into line with what the corporation really is or is becoming. The development of a new corporation name and logo, launching a corporate advertising program, and engaging stockholder relations specialists are a few elements that may figure in maintaining, rebuilding and making more effective a corporation's abiding task of selling itself on Wall Street.

If a company is either in the public eye or dependent on public agencies for decisions affecting its operating environment, then corporate advertising can sometimes be an effective way of portraying the company as a good citizen. However, as with a new product, there can be adverse repercussions if a company advertises itself to the public as something different from what it really is. For example, Joseph Sugarman of JS&A, the direct response marketing concern, developed a creative campaign against what he called the Federal Trade Commission's (FTC's) "vendetta" against JS&A. In a widely circulated catalogue, Mr. Sugarman published a 46-page comic book that told his side of his story. The comic book and other JS&A advertisements encouraged consumers to write to their congressional representatives to get a hearing on how the FTC treated JS&A. A hearing was finally scheduled because thousands of people did write their representatives. However, Joseph Sugarman's defense against FTC charges did not stand up. At that hearing, a congressional inquiry concluded that a lot of the statements in Mr. Sugarman's advertising were false. Thus, Joseph Sugarman's image as outlined in press reports about the hearings is quite different from the picture portrayed in his advertising.

Sugarman's reputation suffered greatly. However, if Sugarman's advertisements were conservative, he would have been in much better shape. This situation is exactly like an advertiser overselling a new product.

Returning to Figure 2-1, this chapter has outlined the three types of roles appropriate for setting objectives for an advertising campaign. These are: causing action, increasing numbers of customers or rate of use, and changing product positioning. Most successful advertising campaigns have integrated all three roles by causing a perceptual change which causes action in terms of either new customers or increasing usage rates.

Summary and Action Questions

- Which customers (potential or actual) will be affected by advertising? How are they operationally defined?
- Is the role the advertising is fulfilling consistent with ethical standards?
- Does the advertising attempt to generate new customers or increase the "use" of current customers? Even image advertising may fulfill this role.
- How specifically is advertising trying to relate to consumer perceptions and preferences compared to competition?
- Are there any consumer misperceptions of your product that advertising could profitably correct?
- Is your product and corporate positioning strategy consistent with your advertising?
- Can advertising roles be translated into operational objectives?
- Are all of your advertising roles consistent with long- or short-term profitability increases for your operation?
- Are you encouraging investigation of new creative roles for advertising?

Further Readings

J. N. Axelrod and H. Wybenga, "Perceptions that Motivate Purchase," *Journal of Advertising Research* (June/July 1985), pp. 19–22. "How to" insights on advertising and positioning.

Robert C. Grass, David W. Bartges, and Jefferey L. Piech, "Measuring Corporate Image Advertising Effects," *Journal of Advertising Research*, 12:5 (December 1972).

Julian L. Simon, *The Management of Advertising* (Englewood Cliffs, N.J.: Prentice-Hall, 1971). How an economist views advertising management.

Notes

1. "Creative Workshop," *Advertising Age* (Chicago: Crain Publications, Sept. 6, 1982), pp. 35–38.
2. F. B. Ennis, "Positioning Revisited," *Advertising Age* (Chicago: Crain Publications, March 15, 1982), p. 43.
3. J. F. Pell, "Winning Products Don't Stress Promotion," *Marketing News* (Chicago: American Marketing Association, March 5, 1982), p. 9.
4. W. P. Margulies, "Street Smarts—How To Market Your Company," *Advertising Age* (Chicago: Crain Communications, May 4, 1981), p. 62.

❖ 3 ❖

Promotion: A Tool in
Market Positioning?

Promotions are by nature short-term incentives intended to encourage the purchase of a product or service. Because of their short-term nature, consideration of the appropriate roles for promotional tools is amorphous in most companies. Many promotions are decided on in the heat of competitive battle. However, before a successful promotion can be launched certain questions should be considered, including

- What are appropriate roles for promotion?
- How is promotion related to pricing?
- Are roles different for consumer and trade promotion?
- What is the relationship between promotion policy, product positioning, and market segmentation?
- What are appropriate roles for both advertising and promotion for new product introductions?

If a competitor's promotion has been able to so affect the sales of a product that quick action must be taken, there is probably something wrong with the rest of the company's marketing mix. A well-positioned product perceived to have benefits to the consumer compared to the competition will typically not need temporary inducements to attract customers from the competition.

An illustration is the U.S. automobile market of the early 1980s. Many of the import cars from Japan are perceived as well-suited to the needs of the American consumer. The cars have the reputation for being economical, durable, and fun to drive. People who have bought Japanese cars tell other people about how good the quality control is. For the most part, the Japanese cars from Nissan and Toyota did not have rebates or promotions during the U.S. automobile recession of 1980 and 1981. However, the big three U.S. automobile makers all resorted to various kinds of promotional devices, including rebates, premiums, and contests, during that period in an attempt to sell their particular products.

In the last decade, promotion expenditures have grown to the point that consumer and trade promotion budgets now exceed expenditures on advertising. Donnelley Marketing's Annual Survey shows promotion budgets in 1984 accounted for 64.4% of total marketing expenditures with advertising accounting for the remaining 35.6%.[1]

Many frequently purchased consumer products that are in the mature phases of their product life cycle are sold mostly on promotional programs. For example, it is estimated that over 80% of coffee sales are due to some type of promotion. The distinction between "price" and "promotion" in some of these markets has been blurred. The use of promotion as a way of decreasing the price to the trade or consumer relative to the competition is quite prevalent. Because some consumers are price sensitive, they will change buying patterns to reflect the brand that is on promotion. The competition then sees sales eroding and reacts with more price promotions. A situation of near constant promotions develops. This high promotion situation is similar to what the economists like to call "free competition," except instead of prices going down, promotion dollars go up. The impact to the consumer is the same, however: the product's net cost is lower. The reason that promotions continue to escalate is that the consumer does not perceive the products within the competitive arena as very different. Hence, firms compete on price or promotion rather than on perceived product attributes.

In this author's opinion, most short-term promotional decisions are really undertaken as a response to weaknesses in other elements of marketing strategy. A key signal that the health of brand within a product class is deteriorating is a continual increase in the promotional budgets combined with little or no change in market share.

Conversely, not every firm is blessed with products and services that have "optimal" positions in the marketplace. In many situations, given the competitive arena in which a firm finds itself, promotions may indeed by the maximal profit alternative. Profitability may actually decline because of increased promotional costs—but it might have gone down even further had the promotional costs not been incurred. As in the case of advertising, promotion must also be justified in terms of its incremental long- or short-term profitability.

This chapter will look at some appropriate roles that sales promotion tools can play. The list of appropriate roles presented here should not be considered conclusive. Creative new promotional devices are being developed every day based on new, creative roles. Choosing among the appropriate promotion roles cannot be done in a vacuum. Here, as with advertising, they must be integrated with corporate and marketing strategies. There are also a number of interrelated roles that promotion can perform at different levels in the marketplace. Promotions can be directed at the ultimate consumer, people in the distribution channel, or the company's salesforce.

Consumer Promotion

Similar to consumer advertising, consumer promotion can also increase the number of customers or increase the rate of use among current customers. The word "consumer" is used here in its broadest sense to mean the ultimate customer of a product or service. This "consumer" may be a business, a household, or any other entity that buys. As with advertising, promotion at the consumer level may also have an effect on the position of the product and may precipitate immediate action. These roles are interrelated and may all be appropriate for the same promotion. Some promotions may only affect one of these roles. However, when planning promotional activity, one must consider the effect of promotion on all possible roles.

There is one role for temporary consumer price reductions or deal promotions that is not shared by advertising. If the retailer has higher inventory storage costs than the consumer, then the retailer might find it worthwhile to reduce price in order to induce the consumer to hold some of the inventory. Some consumers would be willing to carry some inventory if the price is reduced. As Blattburg, Eppen, and Lieberman observe, "A deal is the condition needed to complete this exchange, since consumers cannot be persuaded to hold inventory by a constant price."[2] Figure 3-1 shows how all these roles may be interrelated.

Many price-oriented promotions are justified by their claim to increase the number of new customers for a particular brand. Promotions are seen as inducements to break down brand loyalty to competitors. This role is highly appropriate for new products, but it is probably inappropriate for established products that have been tried at one time or another by most of the participants in a market. Unless the consumer's perception of a product changes as a result of trying the product on a promotional purchase, he or she will not repeat purchase the product when it is no longer on promotion. The consumer will simply return to his or her normal purchasing habits.

It is important to remember that brand loyalty can be fickle. Today, your competitors may be susceptible to breakdown of brand loyalty because of your company's promotions—but tomorrow, the competition's promotions can jeopardize brand loyalty to your company's product. In fact, in those product classes where the great majority of consumer sales are made on promotion, loyalty among all brands may be low. As discussed above, this indicates lack of effective marketing strategies for the brands in the product class.

Recently, fast food marketers began to fret in earnest about

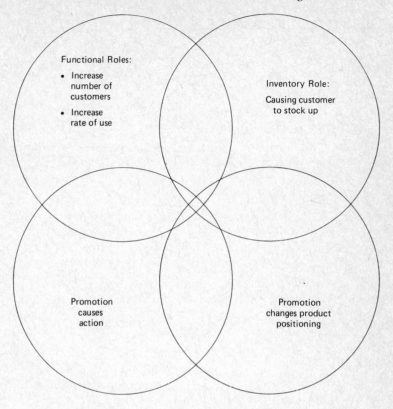

Figure 3-1. Interrelated promotion roles.

the use of short-term consumer promotions, especially coupons. As reported in *Advertising Age*, coupons hit "feverish new heights" in the fall of 1980. Dealing hit a record 9% of total fast food sales, up 17% from the prior year, according to the Crist Marketing Services, an industry tracking company. "The entire industry has taken a trial device and turned it into a crisis management tool," said Arthur Gunther, president of Pizza Hut. "Right now, Pizza Hut is doing more than I'd like. We're working to get away from couponing because it erodes the integrity of your product."[3]

However, couponing in the fast food industry may be increasing the total use of the service by customers. Fast food eating is more of an impulse item than coffee, for example. Thus, rather than affecting market share long term, for many impulse items, promotions may increase their usage and thus the size of the market.

The second role of promotion, increasing the rate of use of current customers, may be more appropriate for some established products. If a consumer already feels brand loyalty, promotions that encourage such loyalty may increase the likelihood that the consumer will be less susceptible to competitors' promotions. In this context, the airlines have developed a creative stratagem. They give consumers free trips depending on the total number of miles or trips flown on each airline over an extended time period. These promotions cause travellers (or travel mode decision makers) to concentrate their trips on a few airlines rather than spreading them out among a number of airlines. Even though American Airlines first started this type of promotion, and all other airlines joined in with similar schemes, the effects of this promotion may not be cancelling like other promotional devices because long-term shares may change. Those airlines that are more likely to meet travellers' destination requirements will probably do better than those airlines that do not have a wide variety of flights. Northwest Airlines had to offer a much more generous scheme for rewarding frequent travellers than TWA, United, or American, for example, because Northwest does not go to as many cities or have as varied a schedule as the other airlines.

There is another role these kinds of promotions play that is not openly discussed in standard marketing textbooks. The company typically pays for the business traveller's trip, but the traveller gets the promotional benefit. Thus, the traveller has the incentive to take the airline that gives the most personal benefits, whereas that airline may not be the most cost effective for the traveller's company. Some companies have recognized this conflict of interest and mandated that all promotional incentives be turned over to the company that pays for the tickets.

In the rental car market, Dollar Car Rental gave green stamps to the traveller. The appeal of this promotion is similar to the airlines' frequent traveller incentive. It supplies the traveller with something extra for renting from Dollar in contrast to Avis or Hertz. This type of promotion in the business market and its attendant conflicts of interests will probably become more important in the future. Cost conscious companies should become more sensitive to inherent conflicts of interest in this type of business promotion.

When coupons or discounts for larger sizes of a product are included with a purchase, they perform a similar role in the consumer market place. Many product managers wishing to justify large promotional discounts on larger sizes of products contend that these discounts get their consumers out of the market and away from competition for a longer period of time. That may be true, but all that is accomplished is that the brand switching is done over long periods rather than short ones. The net effect of these kinds of promotions may still be negative on profitability, but their effects may take longer to see, particularly if the competition reacts with an attractive discount for a larger size product. The consumer may just buy the product having the higher discount. Thus, once the consumer has finished the company's product, he or she may buy another brand.

However, promotion activity on larger sizes may cause buyers to consume more than they ordinarily would, thus increasing market size. For example, larger sizes of soft drinks are typically used up faster per ounce by a family than a sequence of smaller bottles.

The airline promotion mentioned earlier has a productive analogy for other producers by increasing brand loyalty. It may be in the interests of many firms to give promotional inducements to consumers for staying loyal to the firm's products or services. Collecting proofs of purchase from all of a firm's products in order to earn a prize or rebate can be effective, if the competition cannot match your company's ways of meeting consumer needs. The cereal company with more cereals that children like will be more successful in such a promotion than a cereal company with only one minor brand. Many industrial firms use the above promotional concept, but substitute a cash rebate in the form of a quantity discount for the loyalty prize. They may offer a long-term contract to a customer in return for a price concession or rebate. If a firm could combine many of their products into such contracts, those firms with more products that its customers wanted would be more successful. The legality of such arrangements has to be carefully checked.

In general, many of the successful consumer promotion concepts can be adapted to industrial products and services, if top management is open enough to accept new, creative ideas. According to a summary in *Advertising Age*, "Once the province of such mass marketers as Procter & Gamble and General Foods Corp., sweepstakes, contests and games have been introduced into the financial community and the airline industry in recent years, penetrating even such categories as veterinary medicine, agricultural insecticides, lingerie, show manufacturing and heavy equipment."[4]

Trade Promotion

Trade promotions are usually described as temporary inducements to the trade to persuade them to perform particular activities such as increased stocking, display, or consumer price reductions. All the comments made above for consumer promotion about their lack of permanence and relation to weaknesses in marketing strategy apply doubly for trade promotions. Most firms have very little idea of the effect of their trade promotion activity. Because of competitive pressures, the amount spent continues to increase each year. The trade is becoming so powerful in many product categories that the use of trade deals is viewed as a must to keep trade cooperation. Thus, the role of trade promotions in many firms is really viewed as a bribe to the trade given under pressure. These firms give lip service to the deal terms that the trade is supposed to perform in order to obtain the trade deal.

Conversely, some firms are careful about enforcing the performance criteria of their trade promotions. These firms typically have well-trained sales forces who can effectively respond to pressures for leniency. Procter & Gamble is legendary for the quality of its sales force. Therefore, Procter & Gamble is almost always able to get trade cooperation for its products and its promotion requirements. It also helps to have products that the trade needs to have on its shelves because the end consumer wants the product.

Consumer promotions such as coupons may have a bigger role to play with the trade than with the consumer. According to Richard Bogomolry of First National Supermarkets, consumer coupons may have a big effect on the trade's stocking decisions.[5] "Coupons force us to stock products for reasons other than (good) movement," he says. Although his company tries not to be intimidated into stocking a product just because a coupon campaign is under way, he says, coupons often do make a difference. "If 2% to 3% of people come in with a coupon and can't find the product, are they going to get angry at us?" he asks. "It's a significant club." Mr. Bogomolry's comments underscore the need for coordinated roles and objectives for all of the marketing mix alternatives, especially trade and consumer promotion and advertising.

Promotions and Positioning

In the haste of most short-term promotion decisions, the effect of those decisions on the positioning of the product is not always considered as carefully as it should be. Promotion decisions can have a great effect on the perceptions of products vis-á-vis its competition, and, in some cases, promotions may help to change the trade-offs that consumers are willing to make among product attributes. Some promotions may almost be considered part of the product or service that is being performed. For example, promotions, games, and contests are becoming an integral part of the fast-food eating experience for many families, especially for the younger family members. McDonald's without some kind of game, prize, or promotion would not be McDonald's. However, McDonald's does not want to be positioned like Maxims of Paris in the consumer's mind and is happy to be perceived as fun and a bit frivolous.

Some short-term promotions can affect the long-term positioning of a product with respect to its competition. According to Philip Kotler, "When a brand is on deal too much of the time, the dealing dilutes the brand image. . . . In fact, dominant brands should use dealing infrequently, since most of it only gives a subsidy to current users."[6]

Some promotions can aid the positioning of a product by reinforcing the perceived brand image and attributes. Coupons that include a selling message and premiums that are related to the positioning of a product may be appropriate long-term aids in marketing strategy. For example, Avis, along with many other rental car companies, was suffering a sales slump in the first quarter of 1981. Like the airlines, Avis wanted to reward business travellers for loyalty to Avis. Instead of using a discount, they wanted to develop a gift promotion that would make a longer lasting and positive impression, according to George Mead, the Vice President of Advertising for Avis as reported in *Advertising Age*.[7] Another discount "could start to make Avis look like a cheap sell company." Avis decided on Tiffany jewelers as the supplier of the incentive gifts because of their quality image which they felt was consistent with Avis' image as a quality rental car company. The promotion offered a gift worth $12 for one rental, a gift worth $24 for two rentals, and so on through seven rentals. Customers could rent as many times as they liked and could redeem the appropriate gifts. To generate immediate business, the promotion offered two gifts instead of one for customers who rented between April 1 and May 15.

According to Avis management and the Avis tracking department, over 100,000 transactions were made from April 1 through August. Of those transactions, 30,000 were directly related to stimulation provided by the promotion. During the first five months of the program the promotion, which cost $250,000 including postage, production, and gifts, was calculated to have yielded more than $1 million in incremental profit.

The promotion was only successful for some Avis market segments. It was a major success with Avis card holders who had personal accounts and with business travellers with small corporations. Avis did not expect a great response from large corporate travellers because "cards are in corporate names and controllers are not too interested in individuals getting benefits. They would rather get price discounts, so the gifts were not a great incentive." This promotion was a case where, according to the company, there were short-term gains and probably no long-term disadvantages. The image of Avis as a quality rental car company was not harmed. The image might have been harmed had Avis just given discounts for repeated usage of their car rental service.

However, the use of gifts as promotions for loyalty is quite easy for competitors to imitate. Even though the image of Avis was not harmed by the 1981 gift promotion, and it did not harm them long term, their next gift promotion in 1982 brought about a strong competitive reaction. A promotion war similar to a price war erupted in the rental car market with all of the major players attempting to outdo the gifts being given by their competition. Carol Loomis summed up the problem succinctly:[8]

The liabilities of a giveaway battle in which essentially an entire industry is competing are quite obvious. A single giveaway artist may expand his share of the market, managing in the process to offset his added costs. But there is no evidence that giveaways will expand the car rental business as a whole and allow a crowd of corporate big spenders to come out unscarred. Few people, if any, go out and rent cars simply to get a free gift. Unless the customers get that stupid, the industry will have to work at wising up.[8]

Many of the other promotional devices such as contests and sweepstakes, consumer refund offers, allowances to the trade, and price-off packs may have significant long-term risks associated with them because they may erode the position of the product in consumers' minds or invoke an unwanted competitive reaction. This aspect of promotions is ignored many times in the heat of competitive battle. If an unbiased look at your company's promotions shows them to be simple substitutes for temporary price reductions, the role of promotion is probably incorrectly defined and your products are probably not very healthy. If, however, the promotions reinforce the positioning of your products and help insulate the company from competition, then the promotions may indeed be quite healthy. Just as with advertising, an explicit statement of the alternatives and appropriate roles for promotional activities is a necessary first step in productive marketing planning. Senior management should insist on it.

Roles for Advertising and Promotion in the Introduction of New Products and Services

Advertising and promotion may not be necessary for every established product. However, advertising and/or promotion are usually necessary for the successful introduction of new products and services. The usual steps in the new product adoption process offer many appropriate roles for advertising and promotion. All potential buyers, either industrial or consumer, must experience this process for a new product to be successfully adopted. The first step is awareness; the second step is developing an intent to purchase; the third step is finding the product; the fourth step is purchasing it; and the fifth step, depending on the product or service, is repeat purchasing.

Creating Awareness

Advertising is the classic method of generating awareness for a new product. However, sometimes advertising is combined with an appropriate promotional device in order to call attention to the advertising and increase the public's awareness. At the awareness stage, it is important for the consumer to form perceptions of the product that are consistent with post-purchase perceptions of it. This is especially true when the product or service requires repeat purchases to make profits in the long-term.

There are numerous cases of failed products with multi-million dollar development costs. The advertising and promotion for these products generated large amounts of trial, but the products did not live up to the perceptions created. Gablingers beer was brought out five years before Miller introduced Miller Lite. Gablingers had extremely high trial positioned as "the beer that doesn't fill you up." However, after tasting the brew, most consumers did not like it and did not repeat purchase. Gablingers was a colossal multi-million dollar fiasco.

Developing Intent To Purchase

It is not only consumer awareness of a product that is critical. A product must also be perceived as offering some clear benefit vis-à-vis the competition to convince consumers to purchase the product. This intent generation can be accomplished by using either (1) advertising that positions the product effectively or (2) promotional devices that entice the consumer to try the product. Again, if the product stands up after use by the consumer, and will be repeat purchased, a number of these promotional devices can be useful. Sometimes, the most effective promotional device is a free sample of the product itself.

Obtaining Distribution

Assume that the consumer intends to purchase the product, but the product is not where the consumer thinks it should be. The sale might be lost. There is a great amount of synergism between advertising and promotion to the trade and to the ultimate consumer. The trade needs to know that a product will move off the shelves in order to stock it. But for the product to move off the shelves, the consumer must be aware of the product and have intent to purchase it. Without the product being in the right place at the store, the consumer intent will not result in sales.

New Durable Goods and Services

For both consumer and industrial durables, generating trial is the whole objective since people only buy the product once. In this case, the role of advertising and promotion can be to minimize perceived risks and to help foster the diffusion of the new product throughout the target population. Most new products follow a pattern of sales that starts with innovators and then spreads to the rest of the population as they see other people or companies successfully using the product or service. Advertising and promotion can help this process by positioning the product or service in the target consumer's mind as one from a company that has a good reputation and has the appropriate product or service attributes to minimize the perceived risk.

Free samples to influential innovators can sometimes be a very helpful promotional device to facilitate the diffusion of the innovation throughout the target population. This is especially true for medical devices and other kinds of scientific equipment. In these cases, manufacturers sometimes donate the equipment to a research laboratory. The laboratory uses the product and writes it up in articles for the mass market. In turn, laboratory opinions influence the general public.

In many industrial and consumer products, genuine references of people who have used the product or service and found it to legitimately satisfy their needs can be valuable. These references can then be used in advertising. For example, in 1970 a Wharton graduate student, Steven Katz, developed a sophisticated computer program to help bank trust departments keep track of their portfolios. He formed a company to sell the package to commercial banks, but was unsuccessful for a year. Finally, he gave the package to one commercial bank with the provision that the bank could become a reference. The package was successfully implemented at the guinea pig bank. Other banks followed suit once they realized that there was not as much perceived risk in going with a new, computerized approach. The company that was formed aided by this promotion is now SEI Corporation, the largest provider of trust accounting services to banks in the United States.

As we will see in subsequent chapters, just as the role of advertising and promotion is easier to determine for new products and services, the measurement and evaluation of advertising and promotion for new products and services is much easier than for established products and services. There is no prior experience needed to factor out of the effects of the advertising and promotion.

Summary and Action Questions

- Is the firm's product positioning strategy consistent with its promotion programs?
- What roles do the firm's promotion programs play in its marketing mix?
- Can the roles for promotion be translated into operational objectives?
- What's the difference between the firm's promotions and price changes? How does the consumer perceive them?
- What are possible appropriate roles for promotion in the firm's product/service introduction process? Have all of these possible roles been evaluated?

Further Readings

G. J. Eskin, "Tracking Advertising and Promotion Performance with Single Source Data," *Journal of Advertising Research* (February/March, 1985), pp. 31–39. The state of the art in promotion and advertising evaluation.

Ad Tel, Ltd., "How to Test and Measure the Sales Effectiveness of TV

Advertising and Consumer Promotion." New York, 1973. The first instrumented test market for unobtrusively measuring advertising effects.

R. Blattburg, G. Eppen, and J. Lieberman, "A Theoretical and Empirical Evaluation of Price Deals for Consumer Nondurables," *Journal of Marketing* (Winter 1981), pp. 116–120. A very specific statement of hypotheses of the possible functions of price promotions.

B. R. Miller, and C. E. Strain, "Determining Promotional Effects by Experimental Design," *Journal of Advertising Research* (November 1970), pp. 37–42. An example of in market testing and measurement.

R. A. Strange, "The Relationship Between Advertising and Promotion in Brand Strategy," *Advertising Age* (January 10, 1977), p. 44. One person's idea on how advertising and promotion relate.

Notes

1. C. Schleier, "Marketing Image Plots Turnaround," *Advertising Age* (Chicago: Crain Communications, August 15, 1985), p. 15.
2. R. Blattberg, G. Eppen, and J. Lieberman, "A Theoretical and Empirical Evaluation of Price Deals for Consumer Nondurables," *Journal of Marketing* (Winter 1981), pp. 116–129.
3. R. Kreisman, "Fast Food Marketers Decry Couponing Craze," *Advertising Age* (Chicago: Crain Communications, March 9, 1981), p. 6.
4. B. G. Yovovich, "Sweeps and Games Stake Out New Claims," *Advertising Age* (Chicago: Crain Communications, May 3, 1982), pp. m–7.
5. E. Zotti, "Coupons: Food for Thought," *Advertising Age* (Chicago: Crain Communications, April 27, 1982), pp. 5–8.
6. P. Kotler, *Marketing Management*, 4th Edition (Englewood Cliffs, N.J.: Prentice-Hall, 1980), p. 182.
7. "Promotion Roundup," *Advertising Age* (Chicago: Crain Communications, November 3, 1981), p. 16.
8. Carol E. Loomis, "The Rumble in Rental Cars," *Fortune* (Time Inc., March 7, 1983), pp. 93–94.

❖ 4 ❖

Advertising and Promotion/Marketing Mix/Marketing Strategy

This chapter investigates the relationship of the marketing mix to marketing strategy. It then investigates the interaction of advertising and promotion with the marketing mix and, in turn, their impact on marketing strategy. Advertising and promotion decisions are an important part of many strategic marketing decisions. Thus, to make intelligent choices, certain questions must be answered.

- Why are advertising and promotion decisions an important part of strategic decision making?
- How are decisions on advertising and promotion related to other marketing mix decisions?
- Why is the marketing mix many times an integral part of marketing strategy?

When all the jargon surrounding marketing and corporate strategy is taken away, the basic strategic issues all involve resource allocation. Basically, the chief executive officer (CEO) and senior management is worried about products and markets. On which target markets and which products or services should the firm be concentrating resources?

How can strategic resources be concentrated on product/markets? There are at least five different ways (see Figure 4-1) that have been proposed in the literature:

	Current Markets	New Markets
Merger and/or acquisition	☐	☐
Broaden existing product line	☐	☐
Internal new product development		
Change previous allocation for existing products	☐	

(The size of the squares indicates the typical leverage associated with each strategic decision.)

Figure 4-1. How can strategic resources be concentrated on product markets?

1. Merge or acquire a company that has a product established in a current or new market.
2. Internally develop new products for new markets.
3. Extend existing products to new markets.
4. Develop new products for existing markets.
5. Spend more or less on existing products in existing markets or change the marketing mix of existing products in existing markets.

Even though alternatives one through four may be more glamorous, they are not usually directed toward the opportunities available to a firm where there is the most leverage to increase sales and profits over the long term. Most companies are faced with many existing markets and many existing products. The strategic decisions among marketing mix resource allocations in these products and markets can have profound effects on the long-term performance of companies.

However, even when a firm contemplates adding a new product to a market, or a new market to a product, the firm should evaluate the long-term responses to alternatives in the marketing mix for those new product/market combinations. A "vaguely right" approach to these decisions requires answering a number of questions:

- How will the new product be introduced to the existing market?
- What advertising, promotion, pricing, distribution, and product alternatives are there for these introductions?
- What is a good combination of these marketing mix variables? (Typically, the response to different elements of the marketing mix can be aided by knowing the consumers' viewpoint on the market position of existing products and alternative new products.)
- What attributes do consumers use to make their decisions?
- How important are these attributes?
- Are there different "benefit" segments within the market of consumers with different attribute importances?
- How big an impact does the cost structure for producing and distributing products to markets have on some of these strategic resource allocation decisions?

In contrast to the above "vaguely right" approach, most of the marketing strategy approaches proposed by the "strategic" consulting firms are too simplistic for adequate appraisal of strategic alternatives. The evaluation of alternative marketing strategies is too complex a problem to be resolved by two-dimensional analytic representations of the markets and products. Consider, for example, the Boston Consulting Group (BCG) approach. Their approach recommends concentrating on high share, high growth products in large markets. Simply knowing rates of growth, current share, and market size isn't enough to even vaguely determine the long-term effects of changing the marketing mix. The learning curve is used as one justification for the BCG approach. However, the learning curve and all its derivations are not usually very important leverage points for the large majority of existing products in existing markets. When a firm has already produced 30 or 40 million units of a product over 10 years, it is difficult to double production again. In terms of all of their costs, most existing products are quite far down on the learning curve.

Other elements that people have used in these strategy matrices have not been very satisfactory either. Marketing opportunity is one area that has been brought forth as a market attribute that should be considered in evaluating marketing strategy alternatives. However, it is not enough to know that there is a market opportunity; one must also know how that opportunity can be pursued, before a manager can propose such a marketing strategy.

When Philip Morris bought the Miller Brewing Company in the early 1970s, the "standard" marketing strategy approach would have said that this was not a smart diversification move for Philip Morris. Miller beer was then a low-share brand in a slow growth category, the premium beer market. However, the Philip Morris people realized that the problem with Miller beer was its positioning in the minds of many consumers. By doing research, they were able to determine that Miller beer was perceived as a "women's beer." This positioning was eliminating Miller as an alternative in the major market which was the blue-collar, steadier beer drinker. The product was repositioned as a brew that would be suitable for the blue-collar worker at anytime the worker wanted to relax, that is, anytime was "Miller time." This repositioning resulted from an aggressive advertising and promotion campaign that brought Miller beer to a position of leadership in the premium beer market.

Repositioning a product is a key strategic decision that is usually crucial to reviving advertising and promotion productivity. In 1972, Tic Tac was introduced into the U.S. market as a product that would appeal to both adults and children. Adults like the package's convenience and sanitary product delivery. Children found it fun to "Put a Tic Tac in your mouth and get a bang out of life." By 1975, Tic Tac had a 12% market share. Their consumption was broken down into 60% children and 40% adults. However, the major gum companies then began serious promotion of new bubble gums that directly affected Tic Tac's children sales. At the same time Velamints were introduced into the United States as a mint positioned for adults as a strong, sugar-free breath freshener. As reported in *Advertising Age*, by

1979 Tic Tac's share had fallen to 2%, even though Tic Tac introduced several new fruit flavors. According to A. S. Allasia, then Vice President of Marketing at Tic Tac, the strategic decision was then made to reposition the product.

> Mr. Allasia said execs reviewed Tic Tac's original strategy, its reason for being, and finally concluded the company must forego its huge children's franchise (accounting for probably 70% of Tic Tac sales then). Children were too fickle and, furthermore, the product was not intended as a fun item; it was designed as a breath mint, offering convenience and modern packaging, he noted.

> The company decided to move its advertising to Altschiller Reitzfeld Solin/NCK from WRG. The official reason was that "a small fish couldn't survive in a big pond." Other sources have said, however, that Ferrero [president of Tic Tac] placed some blame on the agency for the product's decline, because WRG insisted on focusing on the fun aspect of the mint.[1]

Advertising and promotion were only one element of all the marketing elements needing attention, thought, and research. Tic Tac went about reestablishing the brand as if it were once again a new product. Although the firm had already determined it wanted to appeal to adults with a mouth-freshener story, the agency was left to determine how best to execute that idea.

"Research suggested that many consumers, particularly women, switched to sugar-free mints because of a low-calorie misperception; that they erroneously believed sugar-free mints were also low in calories. The agency set out to set the record straight." As discussed in Chapter 2, if advertising can correct a misperception that is relevant to an important attribute of the buyer's decision process, then the advertising may be effective. The new advertising showed a woman saying she always loved the freshness of Tic Tac but she gave up the taste for fewer calories when the sugarfrees came along. Then the woman learned that the sugar free Velamint had nine calories while each Tic Tac had only one and one-half calories. Not only was advertising to the consumer repositioned, but the trade also had to be reeducated about the new Tic Tac positioning and its sales success. The consumer ads, first tested in Miami, were so successful that by mid-1982 Tic Tac was back at the 9% share level in the 60% of the United States where the repositioned product was rolled out.

Objectives and Strategy

As seen in the next chapter, once a strategic positioning role has been ascribed to advertising and promotion, then the translation of these roles into operational objectives that are directly related to sales and profits can be performed. In the Tic Tac case, objectives related to adult perceptions of Tic Tac's low-calorie attribute relative to a Velamint could be easily related to Tic Tac's sales and profits.

To make a suitable determination of marketing strategy, one must (1) look in some detail at each market and each existing product and (2) ascertain what it is that moves sales and profits in each market. These leverage points are necessary for a true evaluation of strategic alternatives. Rather than using precisely wrong methods for taking very global, quick looks at markets and products, one must evaluate alternative tactical marketing mix activities for each product/market. Vaguely right evaluation of alternative marketing mix tactics is essential for generating effective strategic alternatives that will increase long-term sales and profits.

A Product Portfolio Example

Let's look at an example of the implementation of the vaguely right approach outlined above. This example was disguised to protect confidentialities, but all the numbers and other information are authentic. A health and beauty aids company had seven major products. These products were in different stages of the product life-cycle. Four of the products —Mayflower, Old Ironsides, Independence, and Shenandoah—were well-

established. The other three products—Tenacious, Courageous, and Flyer—were new. The marketing budget on these
seven products was being spent on advertising, trade promotions, and consumer promotions. Top management had continually put pressure on these brands to institute price increases
to counteract profitability problems they thought existed. The
basic strategic problem then was resource allocation among the
seven brands: What should the level of support be for each
brand? What should the marketing mix be? And should there
be any price changes?

Analyses of the relationship of marketing activities to sales
were developed for each brand. The analyses took a combination of three forms:

1. For established brands, statistical analysis of historical data was
   undertaken utilizing any "naturally occurring experiments" (i.e.,
   where different marketing mixes were applied to the brand in
   different regions or time periods). These statistical analyses were
   limited by the naturally occurring experiments. If the brand always used the same percentage of sales on advertising, the
   statistical analysis would not be fruitful. However, if there was
   a lot of variation in the marketing mix, either over time or ge-
   ography, the statistical analysis was quite helpful.
2. For new products, the analyses concentrated on estimating the
   impact of marketing activity on consumer attitudes and behavior. A key focus of the new product marketing mix is on positioning awareness and attitude toward the new product in the
   consumer's mind. This new positioning must then be translated into the trial and repeat relationships that determine long-
   term share for the new product. Based on test market activity
   and pretest market research, the analysis team was able to establish pretty good relationships of marketing activities to long-
   term sales and profits for the new products.
3. Where neither statistical analysis of historical data or models
   linking marketing activity to consumer attitudes and behavior
   were appropriate, management judgment of the needed relationships were developed.

These analyses of the relationship of marketing activities to
sales were put into mathematical models in which various "what
if" scenarios could be evaluated. One of the first factors that

became evident was that there were substantial differences in the marginal response of these brands to marketing dollar expenditure.

Table 4-1 shows the estimated change in revenue dollar per change in marketing dollar for each of the brands for each of the elements of marketing mix: advertising, trade promotion, consumer promotion, and price changes. For advertising, the difference in marginal response ranges from a low of .6 (for Mayflower) to a high of 1.7 (for Courageous and Flyer). In trade promotion, the range is from a low of .6 (for Tenacious) to a high of 1.4 dollars. Note, however, that consumer promotion is not as sensitive to differences among the brands. All the brands seem almost equally responsive to dollars spent on consumer promotions. As discussed previously, if consumer promotion simply induces price- and deal-conscious consumers to switch temporarily among a set of nationally advertised and recognized brands, then their sensitivity to promotion should be fairly similar. Price changes resulted in a moderate difference between the brands. Their sensitivity to prices was shown by their unit sales decline for 1% price increase.

Table 4-2 shows the implications of these marketing sensitivities on various scenarios of alternative strategies for increasing sales or profits. These are just a few examples of the many

Table 4-1.   Substantial Differences in Marketing Sensitivities Were Found

	Estimated Revenue per Change in Marketing Dollar			Unit Sales Decline per 1% Price Increase
	Advertising	Trade	Consumer	
Mayflower	.6	.75	1.5	.7%
Old Ironsides	1.6	.6	1.4	.6
Independence	1.3	.7	1.4	.6
Tenacious	.8	.6	1.5	.6
Courageous	1.7	1.3	1.4	.5
Flyer	1.7	1.4	1.2	.7
Shenandoah	1.2	1.2	1.3	.4

Source: Management Decision Systems, Inc. Disguised case study, Waltham, Mass., 1984.

Table 4-2. There Were Clear Opportunities To Increase
Sales and Profits

Alternative	Total Marketing Budget	1982 Sales	1982 Contribution
A. Base case	$75	$320 MM	$120 MM
B. Reduce spending	65	313	123
C. B + price increases	65	317	126
D. Adjust spending	75	324	123
E. D + price increase	75	330	127
F. Spend more + price increase	82	340	130

Source: Management Decision Systems, Inc. Disguised case study, Waltham, Mass., 1984.

scenarios management evaluated. Note that the base case has
a marketing budget of $75 million, sales of $320 million, and
profit contributions of $120 million. The following alternatives
were evaluated: (1) reducing spending and increasing prices; (2)
adjusting the same level of spending ($75 million) among dif-
ferent brands so that more productive use was made of the
money; (3) adjusting the spending with a price increase; and,
finally, (4) spending more and increasing prices. Note that while
increasing prices was almost never a profitable option, adjusting spending among the brands based on their respective productivity levels for the marketing mix variables resulted in potential for a $3 to $4 million increase in profit.

This vaguely right approach is very different from the consulting firms' matrix approach—that is, just looking at sales
growth and market share. The matrix approach to strategy only
gives a summary of which product market combinations should
be stars, dogs, or cash cows. In contrast, Table 4-2 shows the
outcome of different marketing strategies directly in terms of
sales and profits. There is nothing in any of the general strategy models that generates sales and profits from alternative
strategic allocations of resources.

The two strategic concepts of market share and market growth are only a small part of this vaguely right analysis. Market share is not considered directly in the numbers in Tables 4-1 and 4-2. Instead, it is an implicit factor in how a brand will respond with more or less dollars allocated to its marketing mix. The growth of the particular market will also influence the response of the brand to the different elements of the marketing mix. Market share or growth are not the crucial issues. A key issue in marketing strategy and in advertising or promotion strategy is "Where can the advertising or promotion dollar do the most good in terms of increasing the company's long-term profits?" It is not how to balance share or sales growth. Many other factors are at least as important in evaluating alternative marketing mixes. Product positioning, market segmentation, consumer response to advertising or promotion, pricing, and distribution alternatives are all at least as important as market share and growth. Most companies return profits to shareholders. But do any directly return sales growth or market share? Sales growth and share must be converted to profits for their results to be truly productive.

What happened to the seven products in the example? The company management took a conservative approach to the results of the marketing strategy study. They either held budgets constant or slightly reduced some of them for the least responsive elements. They put more money into consumer promotions for the brands in which it made sense. They increased prices selectively. To give more credence to the judgments and analyses that were made, they initiated an advertising weight test and a promotion test in order to measure more precisely the relationships they had used in their analysis. (Chapters 6 and 7 will discuss the general significance of these advertising weight tests and advertising and promotion experiments.) In the first year in which the strategic program was implemented, the company saw a profit impact conservatively estimated at $2 million. But, of more importance, the company is taking steps (through the use of strategically relevant advertising aand promotion tests) to improve the strategic decision making for future years.

Advertising and Promotion and Other Marketing Mix Variables

Price Interactions

Well-designed advertising and promotional programs reinforce the other elements of the marketing mix. They do not hinder their application. The key consideration is the perception of the product or service in the consumer's mind upon exposure to the advertising and promotion program. This consumer perception should be consistent across all the marketing mix elements. For many products or services, the price of the product is a sign of quality. In the beer market for example, the price of a super-premium beer is one of the ways many consumers determine whether a beer is right for the personality and image they want to project. The advertising and promotional program for a "super-premium image beer" must be quality-oriented and quite dignified. A temporary price reduction promotion that just says "for a limited time only 20% off on every case of this beer" would be contrary to the high-quality, high-price positioning. This type of promotion could ruin the image the company was trying to project even though it would probably cause significant short-term sales gains.

Many mature product classes have resorted to price promotions as a way of increasing short-term sales. Once one firm has started short-term price promotions, other firms within the product class adopt the practice. Soon, most of the product class is being sold only on some kind of promotion or deal. This is really just a way of competing on price for most of the consumers. A category in which 70 to 80% of the volume is done on some kind of consumer promotion shows a lack of well-defined, well-positioned products. In such markets, the challenge is developing well-positioned products and finding promotions that are consistent with the product positioning. This is where the creative "art" of marketing comes into play.

Distribution Interactions

The interaction of advertising and promotion with distribution policies is sometimes quite complicated. In the short run, the better the consumer coverage of distribution outlets for a product, the more impact an advertising or promotion campaign will have. Instead of being displayed at 50% of the stores at which consumers shop, a brand is in 75% of the stores. That is 50% more distribution. Advertising, and promotion programs will typically become 50% more effective because they will have 50% more exposure. This exposure concept only applies to the extent that consumers will not go to a different outlet to find a product that is unavailable in their normal place of purchase. This exposure is operative, however, only in the short term. There are long-term implications of distribution on advertising and promotion that also must be considered.

The character of the outlets in which a product or service is distributed should be consistent with the position that the advertising and promotion programs are portraying. If the distribution channel is not consistent with the positioning, there will be long-term problems with the consumer's perception of the product's position. A good example of this is the Superscope Company after its purchase of the Marantz Stereo Company. Superscope increased the production capacity for Marantz equipment and developed a quality-oriented advertising campaign. However, they also changed the distribution strategy of Marantz from high-quality, specialty stereo stores to stores with broader distribution, including catalogue showrooms and discount houses.

The catalogue showroom stores and discount houses loved having Marantz equipment to sell. They discounted it from the specialty stores and were able to move large amounts of Marantz equipment. The first two or three years of this broadened distribution policy showed a dramatic increase in Marantz' sales and earnings. However, over the longer term, many consumers could not understand how a high-priced, high-quality item such as Marantz would be in their neighborhood discount or catalogue showroom. Marantzs' image started to decay. More important, some high-quality stereo stores decided not to take Marantz equipment because it was available in lower-priced, competitive outlets. Once Marantz became less well-known in the high-priced, high-quality specialty stores, it was no longer as attractive to the discounters.

This vicious circle led to such large sales declines and losses for Marantz that the company curtailed distribution of Marantz. A new line, called Marantz Gold, was developed. It will only be distributed in high-quality specialty stores. However, it is questionable whether this line will ever achieve the success of the original Marantz line. Image problems—stemming from the company's short-term oriented distribution policy—exist with both consumers and high-quality retailers.

Sales Force Interactions

Just as advertising and promotion can help or hinder distribution policies of a company, they can also reinforce or hinder the performance of the company's sales force. For consumer products, trade promotions give the sales people something to talk about with the store buyers during each sales call. According to sales force opinion, there are never enough promotions. Similarly, most sales forces would say that their product is too high in its price to the trade. These common perceptions toward promotion and price are symptoms of products that are not well-positioned in the consumer marketplace.

If a store buyer knows that consumers want a particular brand, that buyer is going to want to have it in stock and give it plenty of prominence on the store shelf. It is only when the store buyer sees a product as no different than the competition that promotions, temporary price reductions, and pricing become important. However, what the sales person should be doing is going over the company's advertising program with the store buyer to explain how the advertising program will cause more pull of the product through the outlets. This is a much more difficult selling task and requires a well-trained sales force. It is a lot easier to come into a buyer and say "look what I can give you free this month," than it is to describe how an advertising program will affect consumer behavior. Promotions directed at the sales force may help motivate desirable long-term behavior. A promotion in which sales reps receive prizes for describing the advertising program or convincing dealers to undertake cooperative advertising may be very useful.

Summary and Action Questions

- If the marketing mix and advertising are considered as part of the firm's resources, on what criteria would the firm's marketing vice presidents be instructed to allocate such resources to the various product/market segments?
- What marketing opportunities should the CEO and senior management attempt to be aware of and how should they proceed with assimilating the alternatives and proposals?
- What can management do to aid in the repositioning of a product or service?
- For which of the firm's products or services and in what element of the marketing mix does consumer perception play a key role?
- Granted, senior executives cannot be aware of every marketing decision that must be made. However, on what areas of the internal marketing decision making process should they be kept informed?

Further Reading

Journal of Marketing (Spring 1983). This issue focuses on marketing strategy and is highly recommended.

G. L. Urban, and J. Hauser. *Design and Marketing New Products* (Englewood Cliffs, N.J.: Prentice-Hall, 1980). An excellent text covering some of the best measurement techniques and management concepts for new product development.

Robin Wensley, "Strategic Marketing: Betas, Boxes, or Basics," *Journal of Marketing* (Summer 1981), pp. 173–182. A good critique of simplistic approaches to marketing strategy decisions.

Yoram J. Wind, *Product Policy, Concepts, Methods, and Strategy* (Reading, Mass.: Addison-Wesley, 1982). An excellent text (especially chapters 1, 4, 5, 6, 7, 17 and 18) which covers product policy with a research-oriented, profitable methodology.

Note

1. N. Giges, "Corporate Close Up," *Advertising Age* (Chicago: Crain Communications, April 19, 1982), p. 4.

❖ 5 ❖

Setting the Objectives

Previous chapters discussed the generation of appropriate roles for advertising and promotion. This chapter discusses the interdependent task of translating these roles into advertising and promotional program objectives. To do this, senior management must be able to answer the following questions:

- Why are operational, measurable advertising, or promotion objectives sometimes inadequate?
- What can senior executives do to make sure that advertising and promotion objectives will affect the firm's sales and profits?
- How valid are many common advertising and promotion objectives?
- What kinds of trade-offs need to be considered in developing and evaluating advertising and promotion objectives?

These problems are interdependent because if a thorough job has been done of analyzing appropriate roles, then the objectives for the advertising or promotion programs are obvious. However, in many cases, analysis of appropriate objectives has redefined the roles for advertising and promotion.

It is currently quite fashionable for management to insist on objectives for all advertising and promotion programs. Typically, these objectives are mandated to be operational and measurable by order of the chief executive officer or chief marketing officer. This insistence on measurability of objectives is fine as far as it goes. It is needed so that all the people involved in advertising and promotion from the top of the corporation to those responsible for implementing the tactics know if they've succeeded.

However, operational, measurable objectives are not enough. As outlined in Chapter 1, many objectives are precisely wrong. The firm must know that they are specifying something relevant to the long-term sales and profits of the product or service when they engage in developing operational objectives. In this author's opinion, it is entirely appropriate and feasible to relate all of the operational objectives a firm uses in measuring its advertising or promotional campaign to long-term sales and profits. There are measurement devices that are both proper and cost-effective for developing these links. Most managers do not presently insist that advertising and promotion objectives be related to long-term sales and profits. Sometimes the linkage between operational objectives and sales and profits are vague or tenuous. However, as long as the linkage can be estimated, the objective may be appropriate. The following discussion analyzes various appropriate objectives for advertising and promotion and shows how they relate to long-term sales and profits. An overview of methods for relating advertising and promotion objectives to each other and to long-term sales and profits will be discussed in Chapter 10.

Alternative Objectives

Figure 5-1 outlines a number of advertising and promotion objectives and their relationship to long-term sales and profits. Some objectives are difficult to relate to these criteria while others relate easily. All objectives, however, whether they relate easily or with difficulty, must be related to long-term sales and profits in order to compare alternative advertising or promotional programs.

For example, most marketers believe that direct response advertising or promotion is the easiest kind of advertising and

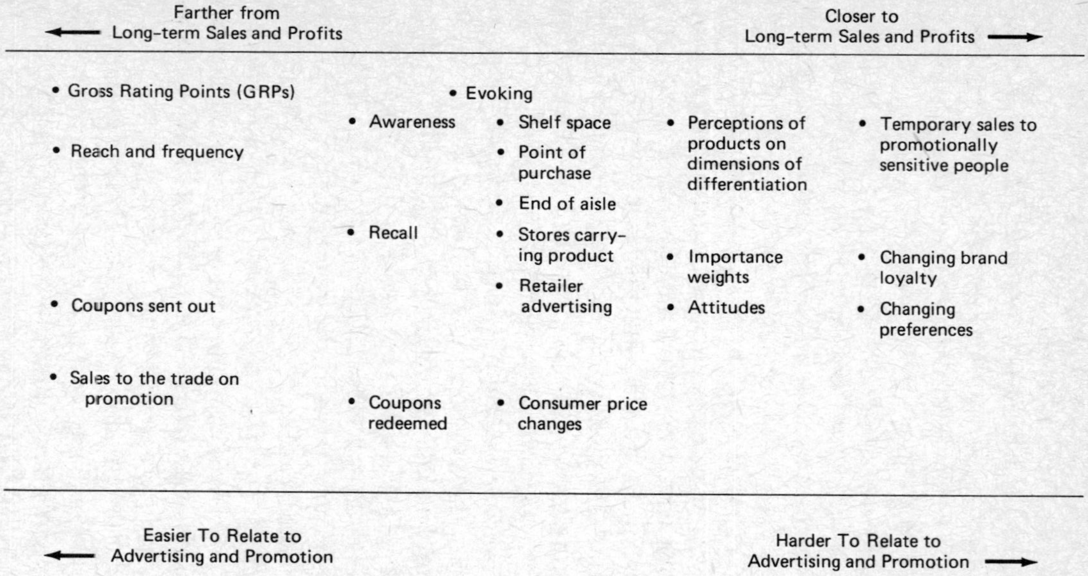

Farther from
Long-term Sales and Profits →

Closer to
Long-term Sales and Profits →

- Gross Rating Points (GRPs)
- Reach and frequency
- Awareness
- Evoking
- Shelf space
- Point of purchase
- End of aisle
- Temporary sales to promotionally sensitive people
- Perceptions of products on dimensions of differentiation
- Recall
- Stores carrying product
- Retailer advertising
- Importance weights
- Attitudes
- Changing brand loyalty
- Changing preferences
- Coupons sent out
- Coupons redeemed
- Consumer price changes
- Sales to the trade on promotion

← Easier To Relate to
Advertising and Promotion

Harder To Relate to
Advertising and Promotion →

Figure 5-1. Alternative advertising and promotion objectives.

promotion to evaluate. In this kind of advertising or promotion, the advertising or promotion actually sells products or services. Finding out whether the program was successful or not seems fairly straight-forward. Just total the sales, apply a profitability factor to that total, and subtract the total advertising cost. But it is not that easy. To most direct response marketers, repeat business from current customers is an important source of long-term sales and profits.

How can one evaluate the worth of a customer brought in by one direct response ad? The sales generated by two ads may be equal, but one of those ads may generate customers having higher long-term repeat sales while the other attracts more trial purchasers. Over time, a direct response company can learn characteristics about their potential market that may be useful in predicting long-term repeat sales. Such items as the media that reached the respondent and the respondent's zip code and demographic characteristics (if they can be obtained easily) can all help in determining the long-term worth of that respondent. By carefully reviewing the actual sales histories of customers in relation to these explanatory variables, a direct response marketer can use them to do an effective evaluation of new advertising and promotion campaigns.

As Figure 5-1 shows, for marketers with various distribution stages, there are numerous objectives available. Although the objectives on the right of the figure are closer to long-term sales and profits, most of the current objectives of advertising and promotional programs (i.e., those objectives that are quite far from consumer sales and long-term sales and profits) are on the left-hand side of the figure. The first set of measures on the left side of the figure are quite common as objectives for advertising programs. Gross rating points and reach and frequency describe measures of numbers of people that were potentially exposed to the advertising program. Gross rating points refer to the total number of potential exposures that were generated by the advertising program. Reach refers to the fraction of the population that was, potentially, exposed at least once to the program. Frequency refers to the average number of potential exposures per audience member. Reach times frequency is equal to gross rating points.

By themselves, these media objectives are meaningless. Unless they have been related to other objectives further to the right on the figure, they tell us nothing about whether the advertising program will contribute to the long-term sales and profits of our products or services. If the gross rating points, reach, and frequency are doing nothing to change consumer behavior from that which would occur without the advertising campaign, then the advertising campaign is not productive. As will be seen in Chapter 8 on media, there is much more to evaluating a media strategy than reach, frequency, and gross rating points. Examples of these other factors include the environment that the media contributes to the advertising and the prestige of the media.

Continuing down the left side of Figure 5-1, coupons are similarly a measure of the media utilized in a promotional campaign. Just knowing that 50 million coupons were dropped says nothing about the effectiveness of those coupons in changing consumer behavior or contributing to a firm's long-term sales and profits.

Trade Promotion Objectives

Again from Figure 5-1, most trade promotions are evaluated by their total sales to the trade in a short-term period. In the heat of a competitive battle, or more frequently in the struggle to make sure that the quarter has good sales numbers, many managers concentrate on short-term promotions to the trade. Here again, unless the actions of the trade in response to these promotional sales change consumer behavior from what would have occurred with different promotions or without promotions, then the trade promotions were not successful. Not only is marketing management judged by total sales to the trade in many cases, but the company's sales force is judged by how well it "loads up" the trade. This may be harmful short-term thinking. Unless these trade promotions are affecting long-term objectives, they may be useless or even harmful to the long-term success of a product.

Fred L. Lemont, an experienced packaged goods marketer and consultant, also criticizes the typical objectives and performance analysis of trade promotion. He uses different words, but his conclusions and action recommendations parallel those in this book:[1]

The difference between how advertising is managed and how promotion is apparently managed is dramatic. Yet, how many systems are you aware of for tracking trade or consumer promotion effectiveness? How much pretesting or in-market testing of trade or consumer promotion did your company carry out last year? How much does your company know about the long-term effect of trade promotion on brand profits?

- In the past 15 years promotion has grown faster in absolute terms than media advertising. Yet, it is still managed much the way it was when it was 5% of the marketing budget rather than 60%. Promotion management techniques have not grown with budgets in the 1970s as advertising management techniques did in the 1960s.
- Some companies consider trade promotion a price discount rather than a marketing expense. If it is not an expense, it literally does not exist and therefore, does not have to be managed.
- Trade promotion is frequently perceived as inevitable—driven by competitive action, trade and industry practice and therefore, uncontrollable.
- Some companies do believe they are measuring trade promotion. The best of these measurements, computerized or non-computerized, detail sales results, promotion period vs. base period. Basically, measurements show you sell more on deal than not on deal. This is sales reporting, not sales analysis.

Trade Promotion and Perceptions

By concentrating on short-term volume objectives, managers may be harming perceptions that affect longer term sales and profit. A summary article in *Fortune* concludes that this harm of perceptions is beginning to be felt.[2]

> The consumer franchise for branded products has indeed been breaking down. A recent study by the ad agency Needham Harper & Steers found that the percentage of people who try to stick with well-known brands dropped from 77% to 59% in eight years. Manufacturers say that the proliferation of trade promotions has helped persuade the consumer to ignore brand and 'cherry pick' products sold at deal prices. If that's true, manufacturers have plenty of reason to worry. In effect, they're undermining the billions they spend on brand-name advertising with the billions they spend on trade promotion.

Awareness, Recall, and Redemptions

If the first four objectives on the left side in Figure 5-1 exist only by themselves and are not related to any variables farther to the right in the figure, then they are examples of precisely wrong rather than vaguely right development of advertising and promotion objectives.

To the right in Figure 5-1 there are three objectives that are closer to consumer behavior but still quite far away. These three objectives—awareness of the product, recall of advertising, and coupons redeemed—are common for advertising and promotion programs. It is easy to measure awareness, recall, or coupon redemption. What is difficult is relating those three objectives to other objectives that are closer to sales and profits. It is not obvious whether recalling an ad, being aware of a product, or redeeming a coupon will have any effect on long-term sales and profits of that product or service. These three objectives are necessary, but not sufficient, conditions for changing sales and profits. If the consumer does not know about the product, it is difficult for him or her to purchase it. However, just knowing that the product exists does not mean that the consumer will purchase it.

In some low involvement, repetitive purchase situations, just being aware of a brand name may be enough to affect sales and profits. However, this can be measured. Similarly, if advertising is to change people's behavior, they should be able to remember the advertising or at least some of the advertising points. Conversely, if the remembered advertising doesn't change behavior, then the recall of advertising is not an appropriate objective. Coupon redemptions are certainly necessary for the success of a coupon promotion, but coupon redemptions are not sufficient for insuring that the promotion has done something to affect long-term sales.

It is much easier to measure achievement of these three objectives than to relate changes in the objectives to long-term sales and profits. However, without the relationship to long-term sales or to one of the other variables that is closer to long-term sales, the use of these awareness, recall, or coupon redemption objectives is not appropriate. Here again, because the objectives themselves are easy to measure, many managers are being precisely wrong rather than vaguely right.

New Product Evoking

For new products or services, the next objective, "evoking," can be very useful. Operationally, evoking means that the consumer considers the new product or service as one of the products that he or she considers as a possible candidate for purchase. It has been shown in a number of new product studies that evoking is a necessary condition for trial. If the relationship to evoking and trial has been developed by previous research, and research has shown the new product to have an attractive position on evoking, then evoking can be a very useful operational objective for advertising and promotional programs for a new product or service.

Other Appropriate Intermediate Objectives

The next group of objectives for Figure 5-1 are all appropriate intermediate objectives for evaluating trade promotions, trade advertising, and sales force activities. Shelf space, point of purchase display changes, end of aisle display changes, changes in stores carrying the product, retailer advertising, or consumer price changes in the stores, are all objectives that may change sales or profits if they are achieved. However, these objectives are not easy to measure or to relate to long-term sales or profits. There are commercial syndicated services for obtaining these measurements, but these sources do not have complete samples of markets and their measurements are sometimes spotty. They are also typically fairly costly. However, they are better than nothing. If one is to look at the value of using these intervening variables as objectives to measure the effectiveness of costly promotions and advertising campaigns, however, the cost versus the value of this syndicated data may be worthwhile. In Chapter 10, concepts for evaluating the cost versus the value of such information will be discussed.

Fred Lemont underscores the costs versus value of measurement of promotions compared to the value of measuring advertising.[3]

Promotion dollars, trade and consumer, are immense. A Donnelley survey of 50 major packaged goods companies, taken in 1979, indicated the average split of the total marketing budget was 40.5% for advertising and 59.5% for promotion.

Of the promotional budget, 34.7% was spent on the trade and 24.8% was spent on the consumer.

Forty of the nation's largest package goods companies spent $4.7 billion in media advertising in 1978. Applying the 1979 Donnelley shares of total marketing dollars to media advertising and to consumer and trade promotion devices, the following total marketing expenditures for these companies add up like this: Media advertising, $4,703,000; trade promotion, $4,030,000, and consumer promotion, $2,880,000.

What this means is that the media advertising portion of that marketing budget receives more attention than trade and consumer promotions. For example, major marketing companies pay up to 15% of their media budget to agencies for the content and management of the advertising dollar, and have large in-house advertising management groups as well.

Also, the marketing company with a $50,000,000 advertising budget probably spends at least $1,000,000 on various forms of measurement and analysis of advertising effectiveness. And, the largest single task of a package goods brand management operation usually relates to advertising.

Contrast this effort with how much the typical major package goods company spends on creative effort, management and measurement of the promotion part of its market. The 60% of the marketing budget.

Positioning Objectives

The next four objectives in Figure 5-1 relate to product or service positioning. Some companies who want to become more "sophisticated" have begun utilizing these objectives for judging advertising and promotion campaigns. Typically, these companies do a research study before the advertising campaign is undertaken to evaluate the positioning of products in the market. They do another study after the advertising campaign has been running to see if either perceptions, dimensions, importance weights, or attitudes have changed as a result of the advertising campaign.

This is fine as far as it goes. However, most firms do not go far enough in utilizing these positioning objectives. If these positioning objectives do not affect sales and profits, it is inappropriate to utilize them. Most positioning research studies have not taken the crucial step of proving that changes in product perception, importance weights, or attitudes toward the product will change sales of the particular product or service. The relationships between these positioning variables and long-term sales or profits are difficult to determine. The measurements usually have a lot of noise associated with them and are not as precise as researchers or brand managers would like. However, the measurements are very useful when compared to the alternative of not measuring at all. If positioning variables are used as objectives without relating them to long-term sales or profits, then management is again guilty of being precisely wrong rather than vaguely right.

Profitable Objectives

The next to last set of objectives in Figure 5-1 is relatively easy to relate to long-term sales and profits. However, these objectives are quite difficult to relate to advertising and promotion campaigns. The first variable, temporary sales to promotionally sensitive people, can be utilized by itself as a conservative measure of effect on sales and profit due to a promotion. In some competitive situations, temporary sales to promotionally sensitive people may justify themselves by the increased profit that is generated from these sales. The decision support systems chapter, Chapter 10, will show an example of how a coupon promotion can be evaluated in terms of both long- and short-term profitability. The key to the evaluation is determining the incremental sales that occurred because of the promotion.

The other two objectives in this group, changing brand loyalty and changing preferences, are at the core of successful advertising and promotion programs. Much research has shown that changing brand preferences and changing brand loyalty are often related to long-term sales and profits. Brand loyalty and brand preference can be measured fairly easily at moderate costs. However, the relationship of advertising or promotion programs to changes in brand loyalty and changes in brand preference is quite difficult to discern. In many cases, field experiments are needed in order to develop these relationships.

Trial and Repeat

The last variables in Figure 5-1 are directly related to changes in long-term sales and profits for new products or services. Trial of a new product is necessary (but not sufficient) for long-term success. Repeat purchases of new products are also necessary

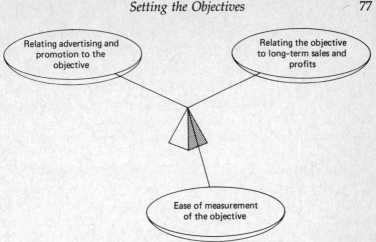

Figure 5-2. Three trade-offs needed to balance advertising and promotion objectives.

for long-term success. If an advertising and promotion campaign is trying to get consumers to adopt a new use for a product or service, then trial of that use is necessary for long-term sales and profit changes.

The relationship of these variables to long-term sales and profits is easily determined. Trying to relate these variables to changes in advertising and promotional programs may be difficult, however. These relationships are typically much stronger and easier to discern for new products, though, because there is little prior consumer knowledge or consumer behavior that muddies the measurement process.

Figure 5-2 summarizes the trade-offs that are made in developing objectives for advertising and promotional programs. These trade-offs involve three considerations: (1) ease of measurement of the objective itself; (2) ease of relating that objective to changes in long-term sales and profits; and (3) ease of relating changes in advertising and promotion programs to those objectives.

As the reader can see, there is no one set of objectives that is easy on all three considerations. Thus, developing advertising and promotion objectives involves trade-offs. A good marketing manager will be one who can find the objectives that are truly the leverage points in delivering the appropriate role for the advertising or promotion program. Chapter 10 will show how these objectives can be measured and how they can be related to each other, the advertising or promotion programs, and long-term sales and profits.

Summary and Action Questions

- Examine the company's advertising objective. Does the objective look at the short run or the long run? Can the results be easily measured? How will the effectiveness of the ad campaign be related back to the company's objectives to see if the campaign was successful?
- Consider reach, frequency and gross rating points. How would knowledge of these statistics enable the firm to make a more sound decision on marketing resource allocation?
- What is the relationship of advertising and promotion to brand loyalty ahd changes in brand preferences? How can senior executives affect this relationship?
- What short-term versus long-term trade-offs should the CEO and senior management be concerned with in order to balance advertising and promotion objectives?

Further Readings

Charles K. Ramand, "One Company's Approach to Measuring Advertising Effectiveness." Reprinted from the Proceedings, 4th Annual Conference, Advertising Research Foundation, New York, 1958. Old but productive case history of how one company measured their advertising.

Ambar G. Rao and Peter P. Miller, "Advertising/Sales Response Functions," *The Journal of Advertising Research* (April 1975). Some nice measurement methodologies with good, practical applications. D. H. Schmalensee, "Today's Top Priority Advertising Research Questions," *Journal of Advertising Research*, (May 1983), pp. 49–62. A summary of conventional wisdom about advertising research.

J. Z. Sissors, "Confusions about Effective Frequency," *Journal of Advertising Research* (January 1983), pp. 33–38. A good discussion of advertising response to repeated exposures.

M. J. Williams, "The No-Win Game of Price Promotion," *Fortune* (July 11, 1983), pp. 92–102. A summary of conventional wisdom about price promotions.

Notes

1. F. L. Lemont, "Room at the Top in Promotion," *Advertising Age* (Chicago: Crain Communications, March 23, 1982), p. 61.

2. M. J. Williams, "The No-Win Game of Price Promotion," *Fortune* (July 11, 1983), pp. 92–102.

3. See Note 1, *supra*.

❖ 6 ❖

Advertising and Promotion Budgeting

Discussion with marketing managers or any random perusal of the marketing trade press shows more cases of precisely wrong answers to the advertising budgeting question than any other area of marketing resource allocation. These precisely wrong answers are a result of management's flight from the great uncertainty they see in advertising budgeting decisions. Some right questions to ask when making such budgeting decisions include:

- Which rules of thumb for budgeting, advertising, and promotion are precisely wrong?
- How is testing related to budgeting?
- How are budgets related to media, copy, and other elements of the marketing mix?
- How can a firm manage the uncertainty of advertising and promotion budgeting instead of running away from it?
- If a firm develops a great new advertising campaign, should it raise or lower the budget?

The uncertainty in advertising budgeting is sometimes replaced with precisely wrong shibboleths. These shibboleths have been repeated to managers for so long that they have become almost believable. To introduce some budgeting concepts, let us investigate a typical, mostly unspoken shibboleth: "If advertising obviously works, raise the budget." Typical scenarios in which this rule is applied include a successful product repositioning when a share decline has been halted (e.g., Miller beer in the early 1970s), the introduction of a successful new product (e.g., Agree shampoo), or a new campaign that executes a strategy better than a previous campaign and causes a change in share (e.g., "Take it off with Noxzema"). In cases such as these, everyone is obviously pleased with the work of the advertising agency and wants to reward them for their successful results. An increase in budget rewards the agency. It also increases the stature of all those involved with the successful campaign because they become associated with a larger account. However, some important questions are often not asked during the budget deliberations following a successful campaign:

- Would we have gotten similar great results if we had spent less (or more) then we did?
- Do we need the same (or greater or less) media weight to maintain the sales momentum of this campaign as we did to start it?

These questions are difficult to answer. They are specific examples of the general questions that management scientists like to ask:

- What is the sales response over time of this product or service to changes in advertising dollars?
- Is this response changing over time?

Every budgeting decision that an advertiser makes requires answers to the above questions. Implicit in the adoption of a new budget is the conviction that it will maximize the long-term (discounted) profitability of the advertising investment. If a manager thought another advertising budget would result in a more profitable sales level, it would have been chosen.

However, as the manager sees the problem, the advertiser cannot answer the question about sales response, because there is little certain knowledge about how sales would react to changes in advertising levels. It is natural for people to shy away from uncertainty. Most managers ignore the problem and rely instead on various rules of thumb. Other common budgeting rules include:

1. To increase share, you must spend greater than the share of the markets' advertising that you want.
2. At least $X per case have always been allocated to advertising.
3. If the advertising investment is lowered, our share will decrease. Share is very important for the long-term health of the brand.
4. At least *x* gross rating points (GRPs) per week are necessary to maintain our presence in the market.

All of the above—and many more "rules" like them—are a means of avoiding criticism. They are safe. Some more progressive managers are beginning to try to manage the uncertainty instead.

How Budgets and Experiments Are Related

The following example (a disguised, but real case) should help to amplify some of these budgeting issues: Assume that a new market manager was just named for a consumer apparel item that was introduced nationally two years ago by your retail chain. The product, one of the most successful in the company's history—reaching sales well in excess of $100 million after two years—has achieved a unique position in the market.

The product was introduced with four 5-week flights of television advertising averaging 300 gross rating points per week in each year. A gross rating point (GRP) is defined as enough advertising so that 1% of the TV homes in the United States would be watching the program. Thus, 300 gross rating points is enough advertising for each TV household in the United States to be exposed three times, or 50% of the households to be exposed six times, or 25% of the households to be exposed 12 times, etc. GRPs thus are a measure of advertising "tonnage."

Most of the multi-million advertising budget was spent on television with a lot of in-store support, especially during sale events. Based on a continued growth forecast for next year and

Table 6-1. Test Schedule

Markets	Apr. 30 to May 20	June 1 to July 30	Aug. 9 to Aug. 25	Sept. 10 to Oct. 20	Oct. 29 to Nov. 18
			Timetable		
Pittsburgh	300 GRP		300 GRP		0 GRP
Cleveland	300 GRP		300 GRP		450 GRP
Houston	150 GRP	150 GRP	150 GRP	150 GRP	450 GRP
Tampa	150 GRP	150 GRP	150 GRP	150 GRP	300 GRP
Detroit	600 GRP		600 GRP		300 GRP
San Francisco	600 GRP		600 GRP		300 GRP
Denver	300 GRP	300 GRP	300 GRP	300 GRP	300 GRP
Philadelphia	300 GRP	300 GRP	300 GRP	300 GRP	300 GRP
St. Louis	900 GRP		900 GRP		0 GRP
Seattle	900 GRP		900 GRP		300 GRP
Atlanta	450 GRP	450 GRP	450 GRP	450 GRP	0 GRP
Kansas City	450 GRP	450 GRP	450 GRP	450 GRP	0 GRP

Source: Information Resources, Inc. Disguised case study (1984).

an increase in media costs per thousand, the agency is recommending a 20% increase in the television advertising budget.

Counting on normal behavior, and relying on the normal rules, the new manager might negotiate with the agency for a 10 to 15% budget increase in order to show a sense of responsibility and the ability to economize if need be. However, this new market manager was more "creative" and "uncertain" that his predecessor. The manager wasn't at all sure if 300 GRPs was a profitable amount to advertise on each flight, or whether 600 or 150 GRPs would be more or less profitable. He wasn't even sure whether flighting was good or not! The manager's only certainty was that television advertising was an integral part of the product's marketing mix.

In order to learn more about the response to advertising for the product, the market manager held out 12 markets (out of 150) to be used for a 7-month-long test of alternative advertising budgeting and flighting strategies. The rest of the markets followed the normal 300 GRP flights that the agency had been recommending. The design of the test is shown in Table 6-1. GRP levels from 150 (half the normal level) to 900 (three times the normal level) both flighted and level were applied to the selected markets. The choice of which market received a particular treatment was done randomly.

Contrary to everyone's expectations, after five months there was essentially no difference in any measure of sales—growth, market share, share of store sales—that could be related to the widely differing levels of television advertising. Five months was a much longer period than the typical purchase cycle for the product. Even during a period when the television ads were trumpeting a 20% off price reduction for a limited time only, sales growth compared either to a pre-period, the prior year, or the total store sales was just as good with 150 GRPs support as with 900 GRPs! Figure 6-1 shows typical results for one measure of sales growth. Each point on the graph is an individual store. Note that there was a wide variation in the sales performance of each store, but that the variation was not associated with the levels of television advertising. Multivariate statistical analysis of other possible confounding factors showed that in-store promotion was highly associated with sales success for this product, but that there was no reinforcing sales effect on this in-store promotion because of higher or lower levels of television advertising. The last three months of the test were refined as indicated in Table 6-1. The 600 GRP and 900 GRP test levels were zeroed and four markets had their television ads eliminated completely. This time the results were not unexpected. The stores in markets having 0, 300, and 450 GRPs had approximately the same sales results!

A plausible hypothesis generated from the testing was that the television advertising campaign was no longer working. It had evidently done its job so well that all that was needed was in-store reminders to keep purchases up. Long-term results of no television advertising weren't available from this test, but as long as some zero TV markets were held out in future advertising campaigns, the company could diagnose these effects. The advertising strategy for the next year was changed significantly based on the tests. The normal strategy became very low (100 GRPs) television advertising, with some test areas at zero and

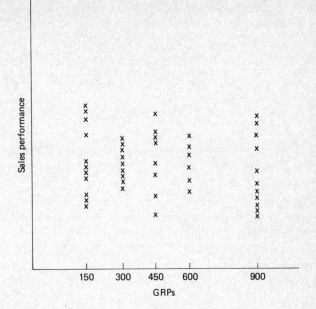

Figure 6-1. Levels of advertising pressure.

some at higher levels. In this way, the manager could (1) continually reevaluate the sales effects of options for the future and (2) estimate the long-term effects of lowering the television advertising budget.

The cost of the continued testing in this real example is not trivial—in the low six figures annually depending on how the accounting is done. However, that cost is more than offset by a savings of millions of dollars in reduced ineffective advertising.

When Warner Lambert Co. bought Entenmann's in 1978, management used market tests to see which marketing roles advertising might fill.[1] Warner Lambert's marketing strategy was to expand Entenmann's by adding to its geographical distribution area. By the end of 1980, Entenmann's products were available to 30% of the U.S. population, compared with 19% at the time of acquisition, and sales had increased 67%. According to William Grove, then the Director of Marketing,

> The company plans to use advertising as needed. We are considering running ads in our older markets, but right now the emphasis is on the new markets where we need to build product awareness the quickest.
>
> Once Entenmann's has been established in a market, word of mouth comments on the products taste, freshness, and quality seem to work quite well in supporting sales with little advertising. In the new markets, the word of mouth process gets a boost from advertising.
>
> "We wanted to get awareness of the product in new markets to a higher level more quickly," says Mr. Grove. "That's why we went to TV outdoor boards and newspapers. We tested TV in Cleveland and it was successful. Now we're running it in Chicago and Atlanta."

Once Entemann's reputation for quality was established, the company evidently was to broaden its product line by relying only on point of purchase displays—with no consumer advertising. Entemann's also introduced the concept of a snack-and-treat aisle display aimed at the impulse purchase of sweet baked goods. That idea, too, seems to be doing quite well.

Testing Trade-offs in Advertising Budgets

As these examples illustrate, the basic problem in advertising budgeting is the determination of the sales response relationship between advertising dollars and sales dollars generated by the advertising over time. Aside from experimenting, another way of trying to solve this problem is to have experienced managers directly estimate the sales response relationship. Managers may use knowledge gained by marketing research and experience with the brand to make vaguely right judgments of different levels of sales at different levels of advertising. However, most manager's estimates are both uncertain and inaccurate. The logical reason for these inaccuracies is that most of the estimates are based on the manager's intuition about the brand's reaction to advertising. However, over the brand's history little has been systematically done for the sole purpose of improving the manager's intuition about sales response to the product.

In fact, there has been a large upsurge in complex econometric research in advertising effectiveness. Econometric research utilizes statistical analysis of advertising, sales, environmental, other marketing activities, and competitive data to estimate a quantitative relationship between sales and advertising over the time periods considered. Econometric methods attempt to mathematically isolate naturally occurring advertising experiments that affect sales. This type of research tries to separate the real sales effects of advertising from the effects of the various rules of thumb relating advertising to sales and other marketing and competitive variables. The conclusions of this econometric work are controversial. Unless the naturally occurring experiments that the econometric models are analyzing provide experience with really different levels of advertising, they will not be as precise as a typical manager would like.

How is a manager to develop estimates of what sales would be at different advertising budget levels if budgeting has always been done at a certain constant fraction of the brand's sales over time? Wouldn't the manager's intuition be better and the estimates more accurate, if he or she had experience with many different budget levels? "Sure," the manager answers, "but if I change advertising budget levels all the time, I'm not going to be as profitable as I would be if I followed my normal budgeting rules! My career path is not happy when my brands don't do as well as they normally do in sales or profits." This is typical short-term managerial thinking.

For the long-term health of a brand it is worthwhile to spend some seemingly inappropriate funds this year, in order to improve the profitability of decisions that will be made in future years. The modern marketing/advertising professional should be continually testing alternatives for elements of the advertising campaign. This testing costs money in two ways. There are out of pocket costs for designing and implementing the tests, gathering the data, and interpreting the results. The tests are also implicitly costly because they involve doing something different with the advertising than would normally be done in some market(s). Theoretically, sales in the market(s) being tested will be different from other normal markets, and thus different profits will result. If the manager believes that the normal policy leads to the best profits for the brand, then changing the policy for test purposes will be costly because of lower profits. Thus, a key task of a manager is developing a balance between the costs of testing and associated research this year and the increased profits in following years that might accrue from the activity. This balance is not usually struck for four reasons: (1) because of most companies' short-term oriented managerial policies; (2) possible advertising agency support for the status quo; (3) difficulty in estimating the elements to balance on the scale; and (4) problems in developing and implementing effective tests of alternative advertising plans.

This chapter will discuss the first three reasons for management not achieving an appropriate balance between the costs of testing and research this year and the increased profits in following years that might accrue from the activity. Discussion of problems in developing and implementing tests will be covered in Chapter 10 on decision support systems.

Short-term Orientation

In most firms, marketing managers are judged on the yearly (or more frequent) sales and profit performance of the product(s) under their control. If they are successful, they are quickly promoted to work at either a different level in the firm or on a larger, more prestigious product. Explicit recognition and weight is rarely if ever given to the value of increased knowledge of a brand's reactions to advertising obtained by testing in management objectives or decisions on career advancement. However, managers would probably do more testing and experimenting if they thought they would be remunerated based on a brand's cumulative profits over the next 10 years instead of just this year's. How many management by objectives programs give real weight to the value of learning this year in order to manage the brand more efficiently in future years?

Advertising Agency Opposition

A hurdle most marketing managers have to overcome to implement useful (as opposed to cosmetic) advertising testing programs is the possible opposition of some advertising agencies. Because of the real uncertainty about the sales effectiveness of alternative budget levels, some agencies may find it easier to maintain their own revenue and profit goals by supporting most of the rules relating advertising budgets to a fraction of sales for the brand.

Any testing of alternative budgeting strategies could cause significant changes in agency revenues. Many agencies support tests of increasing advertising, fewer support tests of decreased advertising. Kenneth Longman, who spent 10 years with a large Madison Avenue agency, wrote a very interesting academic text on advertising.[2] However, even with his academic hat on, Longman's agency orientation crept into his discussion of advertising budget tests. Longman feels that only a few research methods are now available that are helpful in budget-setting. For instance, efforts are continually made to test budget levels by direct experimentation in the marketplace. This is usually accomplished by overspending in a small number of test markets and then setting up a system for tracking sales, awareness, attitudes, and trial in these markets and in a set of control markets (i.e., markets where the usual spending level is maintained). Some more sophisticated agencies will not support even this type of test. What if the higher levels of advertising produce no increases in sales effects? Doesn't that cause some suspicions as to the possible effectivness of the normal budget level? Of course it does!

To continually measure the effectiveness of the current campaign, some test market(s) or area(s) should not be exposed to the advertising, so that the relative sales effectiveness of the campaign can be monitored continually. But many firms do not do this.

Balancing Costs and Value of Testing

Determining the "correct" amount of money to spend on testing and research is a difficult problem. No test or research process gives certain results. The precise mathematical treatment and estimation of uncertainty in testing and research outcomes and integrating this uncertainty into optimal testing plans are intractable for most reasonable problems. The basic idea in the evaluation of testing is that after-the-fact-testing is only valuable when management changes its decision because of the results of the testing, and the after-testing decision is indeed more profitable. The more uncertainty there is on the outcomes of alternative decisions and the more certainty there is in the validity of the test results, the more valuable testing is. Based upon our observations of the results of testing in practice, we believe that most managers aren't testing enough by a factor of ten. After well-designed, well-executed, and well-analyzed tests, the majority of managers seem to change their advertising decisions just as the manager did in the apparel test example that introduced this chapter. This change of decisions implies that the manager's prior uncertainty about the effects of advertising variables was quite high.

One firm that has been using the adaptive testing and experimentation approach for many years is Anheuser Busch, Inc. Ackoff and Emshoff documented how this methodology simultaneously helped the firm increase total sales and profits while decreasing their advertising costs per barrel.[3] It is no coincidence that Russell Ackoff, a management scientist, has had a long-term relationship with top management of Anheuser Busch for these same years. Many chief executives never develop a long-term relationship with a management scientist who can help structure appropriate testing and measurement programs.

Advertising Budgets Related to Sales Response, Media, Copy, and Other Marketing Mix Elements

Budgets and Sales Response

As seen above, the determination of a rational advertising budget is predicated on evaluating sales response to alternative spending levels. The appropriate amount to spend on advertising depends (as the micro-economists tell us) on marginal revenue and marginal costs. How much more sales over time does an incremental $1 of advertising buy? If the incremental profit on the incremental sales is greater than the $1 advertising costs, then the economists tell us to spend the dollar. In the real world, however, it's not that simple. Most managers are correctly uncertain over this incremental sales response. They do not know it precisely at all. They are certain, however, that if they spend another dollar on advertising, that dollar will have to be subtracted from whatever the incremental response is. Thus, in a situation where a manager is certain of spending a dollar, but not certain of getting that dollar in profit back to pay for it, the manager should rightfully spend conservatively. The manager is adjusting for risk by being conservative.

The basic shape of the sales response to advertising relationship is not similar for all products and services. In some cases, the advertising may not be working at all so the relationship is flat. Sales are the same no matter how many advertising dollars are spent. Even for advertising that is changing sales, a saturation point will eventually be reached. That is, there is some point where incremental advertising will no longer be productive. In other words, the advertising has already performed its function and spending more advertising dollars will not cause new changes in consumer behavior.

Differences among products and services in the shape of the relationship curve occur at the lower amounts of advertising spending. Many observers are not sure whether there are increasing or decreasing returns with relatively low advertising budget levels. Figure 6-2 shows one curve (Curve A) with increasing returns at low levels (the familiar S-curve), and one curve (Curve B) with returns that continue to decrease as advertising spending is increased. Those observers who believe that there are increasing returns in the beginning (Curve A) believe that it takes a certain amount of dollars to penetrate the competitive noise level before advertising begins to really take effect. The proponents of decreasing returns (Curve B) believe that advertising is always skimming the cream as the first exposures get people who are more ready to take action than the second exposure, and so forth.

If a manager believes the advertising response relationship is of the S-shaped variety, it can easily be shown that it is not optimal for the manager to set the advertising budget on the lower part of the S. Figure 6-3 shows a dotted line between the O advertising point and point b, where a dollar of advertising begins to get decreasing—rather than increasing—returns to scale. The point where rational budgets should be set is either at O (i.e., it doesn't pay to advertise the product at all) or higher dollars than shown at point b (i.e., where increasing returns stop). The reason for this is simple. Before b dollars are spent, every dollar spent has more response than a dollar previously

Figure 6-2. Two alternative sales-advertising relationships.

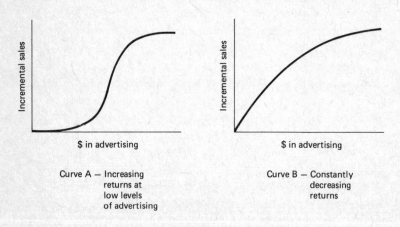

Curve A — Increasing
returns at
low levels
of advertising

Curve B — Constantly
decreasing
returns

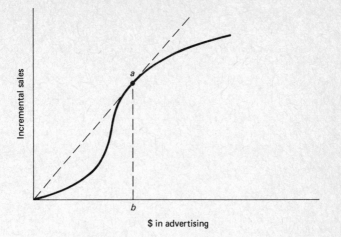

Figure 6-3. Optimal budget levels.

put in. Thus, if it paid, on a sales response basis, to put in the prior dollar, it would pay more to put in the next dollar. The manager can either afford to spend nothing or spend at least *b* in terms of dollars in advertising. The optimal budget is at the point above *b* where marginal revenue equals marginal costs. As discussed above, the manager may want to lower this point to adjust for uncertainty.

Budgets Related to Media, Copy, and the Marketing Mix

Typically, sales response relationships change if copy strategy, media strategy, or other elements of the marketing mix are changed. Some changes can cause the response relationship to become more or less efficient by making dollars work harder or easier. For example, a new media buying strategy might make $1 do the work that $1.10 used to do. This causes a shift in the sales response curve, but no change in the saturation level. Let us call this type of change a +10% efficiency effect. Figure 6-4 shows the influence of efficiency effects on a sales response relationship. The kinds of phenomena that would cause these ef-

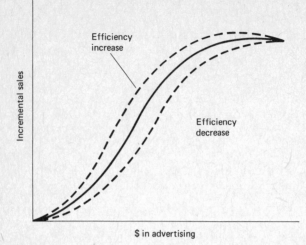

Figure 6-4. Efficiency changes in sales response.

ficiency shifts include changes in media costs, different place-
ment in the same media, or copy changes that cause people to
pay better attention to the advertising, but cause the same consumer behavior as the prior copy.

Another type of change in the sales response relationship is
termed a scale effect. A scale effect causes sales to increase or
decrease on a constant percentage basis no matter which advertising level is considered. A +10% scale effect says that 10%
more sales will results for all levels of advertising. Figure 6-5
shows sample scale effects that can occur in advertising-sales
relationships. These scale effects all have to do with changing
the ultimate saturation level. New media usage that gets a different market segment may cause scale effect changes on the
response relationship. Any copy that repositions the product or
talks about new uses may cause changes in scale effects. For
many convenience products, changes in distribution that allow
more or less people to see the product at their usual store will
cause a change in scale of the response relationship. This is so
because more or less people will be in the market for the prod-

uct. For these products, being in 10% more stores usually implies 10% higher sales for the same advertising dollars. Typically, a change in price or a price oriented promotion will also show scale effects. Changes in a competitor's ad budgets may make it easier or more difficult to get to the saturation level, but will generally not change that level. Thus, competitive budget changes may be associated with efficiency effects rather than scale effects.

Many changes in sales response relationships are combinations of efficiency and scale effects. For example, a copy change may both reposition the product to attract more people in its target market (scale effect) and make it easier for the advertising to do its work by getting more people to pay attention (efficiency effect). Thus, a combination of the effects in Figures 6-4 and 6-5 would occur.

If the manager can isolate the specific type of effect, he or she can make reasonably intelligent estimates of what to do to the advertising budget. In a situation where the changes to the

Figure 6-5. Scale changes in sales response.

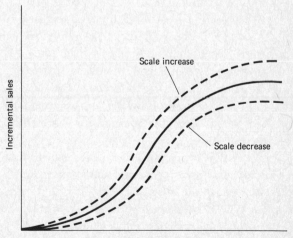

advertising are scale effects such as these in Figure 6-5, it is clear that increases in the scale of the curve should be associated with increases in advertising budgets and vice-versa. For example, a positive scale change means that an incremental dollar of advertising that used to bring in $1 of profit will now bring in more than $1 of profit due to scale changes. Thus, the advertising budget can be increased.

For the increases in efficiency effects such as those in Figure 6-4, it is not as clear what the implications are for advertising budgeting. For most cases, an increased efficiency of a campaign should be associated with a decrease in the advertising budget. However, depending on the exact shape of the curve and the dollars involved, this may not always be the case.

For the curve in Figure 6-6, assume a dollar was the optimal amount to spend on advertising. The slope of the response curve for point *a* is indicated by the line tangent to the curve at that point. This slope represents the marginal or incremental sales dollars per dollar of advertising at that point. In other words, the optimal point is where the incremental revenue just equals the incremental costs (including advertising) for producing that revenue.

If the response curve changes to that represented by the efficiency increase curve, then the optimal advertising budget is lowered from *a* to *b*. At budget level *b* the slope is equal to that of level *a* on the original curve. Similarly, if the response to the advertising achieves an efficiency decrease, then the optimal budget is raised to point *c*. In the great majority of cases, the implications for budgeting follow the implications of Figure 6-6: for efficiency increases, lower the budget; for efficiency decreases, raise the budget.

Now that we have developed the analytical machinery, we have a way of rationally answering questions that constantly plague those people who are involved in approving advertising expenditures. Consider this example: The advertising agency has just developed some great new copy. Copy tests and the manager's judgment indicate that the new copy is significantly better than previous copy. Should the advertising budget be in-

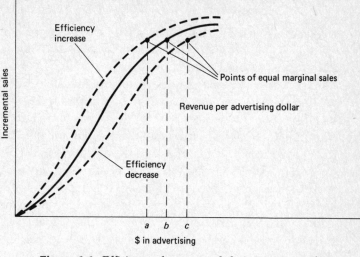

Figure 6-6. Efficiency changes and their impact on the optimal budget.

creased or decreased as a result of this new copy? The analysis above shows that it depends on the role that the copy change is playing. If the copy is getting new people or new uses or doing something that changes the scale of the response curve, then such a copy change would imply an increase in our advertising budget level. However, if all the copy is doing is getting people to pay more attention, but not changing the scale of the curve, it's more than likely that such a copy change would imply a decrease in advertising expenditures.

On the other hand, the more typical situation when media costs rise (which implies an efficiency decrease), does usually support a budget increase. This happens because of inflation.

Other Precisely Wrong Advertising Budgeting Methods

The vaguely right approach described above will now be compared to some common budgeting methods. These methods include objective and task, competitive parity, percentage of sales, and affordable.

The objective and task method involves setting operational objectives and then budgeting enough money to fulfill those objectives. Typical objectives for this method might be to increase awareness by 10% or increase advertising recall by 20%. This method is used by many managers because they feel it is rational and easy to tell whether or not the advertising budget has attained its objectives. However, the big flaw in this approach is that typically no one translates the objectives into their sales and profit consequences. Why is 10% awareness increase the appropriate amount? What if anything, will happen to sales and incremental profits due to the advertising campaign? Awareness and recall can be used as intervening variables to help develop sales response relationships. They can also be checkpoints to determine whether or not the advertising budget is fulfilling its mission. But the intermediate objectives cannot determine budgets by themselves. They must be related, either implicitly or explicitly to sales and profits.

The competitive parity method implies basing the advertising budget on a ratio to that of the competition. This method is only appropriate in some special circumstances, such as where all the competitive players have similar sales response relationships and similar advertising effectiveness. In some cases, for example, one of the firms may have advertising that is doing virtually nothing and their dollars are wasted. In other cases, a firm with effective copy and good marketing strategy supporting it may profitably spend much more than its competitive share. The competitive parity approach is no substitute for critically analyzing and testing the sales response anticipated by changes in advertising budget levels.

Similarly, advertising at a constant fraction of sales or a set amount per case sold is also inappropriate. This budgeting approach assumes that advertising is a cost of doing business rather than a possible contributor to increased sales. The sales forecasts that are typically used to get advertising budgets based on percentages of sales (i.e., last year plus 10%) do not take into account changes in the marketing mix or changes in the advertising budget. These sales forecasts are not appropriate guidelines for advertising budgeting or other marketing mix allocation.

The percentage of sales approach is similar to the affordable approach. In both approaches, only what management feels is an appropriate amount is spent on advertising. Other monies are distributed as profits or invested. However, if the firm is in business to maximize long-term profit, then the affordable approach or the percentage of sales approach is not usually appropriate. There is no direct relationship between what is affordable and what level maximizes long-term profits.

Promotion Budgeting

All of the concepts that have been put forth in this chapter for advertising budgets are also appropriate for promotion budgeting. Most promotion budgets are developed based on rules of thumb that are not related to the long-term profitability of promotion investment dollars. More testing and evaluation of promotion budgets are in order. Few firms evaluate (or even consider) the costs and benefits of extensive testing of alternative promotion budgets. Most outside promotion suppliers and agencies support the status quo. If anything, the problems and lost opportunities for profits in present promotion budgeting methods are more extensive with promotion than with advertising.

Industrial Advertising and Promotion Budgeting

This chapter's message applies even more to industrial advertising and promotion budgeting decisions than to consumer budgeting decisions. The cost of testing industrial advertising and promotion programs is much less because many industrial products and services have directed distribution so that each customer can be a separate test observation. Precise estimates of the sales and profit effects of different advertising and promotion programs can be easily developed with relatively few test customers. Also, because industrial media are more easily targetable, the advertising tests can be more easily implemented. Split run print ads or direct mail programs are easier and less costly to set up than equivalent consumer TV tests.

Whether the advertising and promotion budgets are for consumer or industrial products or services, the CEO and senior management can no longer settle for traditional precisely wrong methods for budget setting. Since a firm's standard budgeting methods have generally been in place for years, it is the CEO who must set new standards. Ideally, this chapter has given the chief executive officer and senior executives ammunition to use in questioning the firm's current methods of advertising and promotion budgeting and—more important—guidance on ways to improve the budgeting process.

Summary and Action Questions

- What is the importance of sales response and advertising? How are they related?
- What does a brand reaction to advertising say about the advertising campaign? Is advertising a panacea for a sick product?
- Should managers accept poor returns in the current period with the expectations of future profitability? How can they convey this idea to upper management?
- What are the manager's incentives to operate at lower profit or sales levels in a period?
- What can the CEO do to help the manager develop a balance between the high costs of testing and market research and the expected increase in future profits?
- How can a manager deal with the possibility of an agency's potential bias away from a decision to decrease the firm's advertising budget?
- What are the different advertising sales response curve scenarios that are possible in the market? How might they affect the budgeting decision?
- How does the firm's current method of advertising or promotion

budgeting compare to those discussed in this chapter? Which of the current methods is it most like? Can it be improved to be more vaguely right?

Further Readings

D. A. Aaker, and J. M. Carmon, "Are You Over Advertising?" *Journal of Marketing* (August 1982), pp. 56–69. An excellent article summarizing facts and concepts which support the thesis that advertisers in general significantly over spend. Every CEO should read this.

J. C. Bucknell, and R. W. McIsaac, "Test Marketing Cookware Coated with Teflon," *Journal of Advertising Research* (Spring 1963), pp. 2–8. A well-executed advertising experiment with management decision value.

J. D. C. Little, "Aggregate Advertising Models: The State of the Art," *Operations Research* (September 1979), pp. 629–667. An excellent summary of what we know and don't know about how advertising at the macrolevel works.

J. L. Simon, and J. Arndt, "The Shape of the Advertising Response Function," *Journal of Advertising Research*, (August 1980, pp. 11–28. These authors marshall data to show that in general there are no increasing returns to scale for advertising expenditures.

Notes

1. B. Holland, "Entenmann's on the Rise," *Advertising Age* (Chicago: Crain Communications, April 27, 19), pp. 531–522.
2. K. Longman, *Advertising Management* (New York: McGraw Hill, 1971), p. 171.
3. R. L. Ackoff, and J. R. Emshoff, "Advertising Research at Anheuser Busch, Inc. (1963–68)," *Sloan Management Review* (Winter and Spring 1975).

❖ 7 ❖

Copy Decisions

Senior management is not generally involved in the act of creating copy or art for advertising and promotion programs—nor should they be involved. Senior managers are not paid to be artists or copy writers. However, it is the top management's job to institute and oversee a process whereby the best possible (i.e., most profitable) programs are created. Therefore, they should know the answers to these questions:

- How important is copy?
- How should the creative activity be structured, managed, and evaluated?
- How is testing related to the creative process?
- How can management improve the validity and reliability of copy tests?

This chapter will discuss alternative methods for managing, structuring, and evaluating the creative process. First a structure for the process is proposed. Then management of each of the elements, including creative generation, relating creative output to the existing strategy and objectives, and pre- and post-testing the creative output, are discussed. As in other areas, there is much room for management to improve the long-term profitability of the creative process.

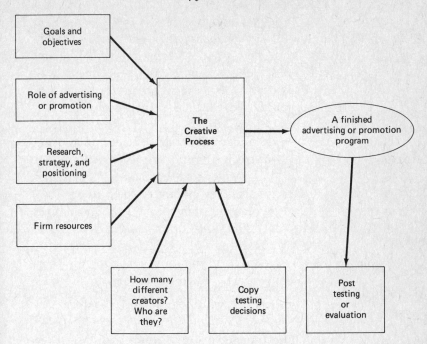

Figure 7-1. The creative system.

Elements of the Advertising and Promotion Program Creation Process

Basically, the program creation process can be viewed as an input/output system. The inputs to the creative process are (1) prior decisions on the role of advertising or promotion, (2) the goals and objectives for the program, (3) all of the thinking, strategizing, and research leading to the statement of objectives and goals, and (4) the firm resources (i.e., compensation, people time, and production expenses) that support the process. The ultimate output of the process are the advertising and promotion programs that will be executed. Figure 7-1 shows this conceptualization of the creative system.

Previous chapters have discussed the generation of appropriate roles of advertising and promotion, positioning, and marketing strategy. All of these management decisions are highly interrelated with the creative output of copy for advertising and promotional programs. If the positioning of the product is well conceived, then mediocre creative execution of that positioning may be successful. Conversely, excellent creative copy can rescue a mediocre positioning strategy. There is real synergy, however, when market and positioning strategy, advertising objectives, and excellent creative output are combined.

Miller Lite's management knew that they had to properly position their dietetic beer before they introduced the product. Their goal was to convince the predominantly male, heavy beer drinker that it was manly—not "sissy"—to drink a diet product. The funny, memorable advertisements with sports celebrities clowning around created exactly the right image for the beer. These Lite beer commercials created a new era in the beer market.

The Importance of Copy

Before discussing how top management can affect the creative process, the importance of copy should be reemphasized. Advertising and promotion copy is the final execution of the planning, strategy, and positioning of the product or service. Of the three advertising and promotion decisions—budget, media, and copy—copy is by far the most important. No matter how much is spent or which media are used, an ineffective campaign will remain ineffective. The Delorean motor car was introduced into the U.S. market with a sizeable advertising budget in media to which its affluent market was exposed. However, the ad copy did not give those consumers a compelling enough reason to go to a showroom and see the car. The Delorean introduction failed because of a combination of ineffective copy and an ineffective positioning strategy.

What the advertising or promotion campaign says is more important than where the campaign is executed or how often the program is run. There are a number of instances where new copy has significantly effected the sales and profits of products and services. Many of the examples discussed so far—Tic Tac, Miller High Life and Miller Lite, Entenmann's, Noxzema ("Take it all off"), and Avis ("We Try Harder")—show how powerful copy can be. This excellent copy can come from either strategy and positioning or creative execution of a positioning strategy or a synergistic combination of both positioning and execution.

In the late 1960s, Quaker Oats did research and knew that they wanted to position Life as a good tasting, nutritious cereal. It wasn't until they introduced the "Mikey Likes It" campaigns, however, that Life sales lived up to their potential. This effective campaign has been used since then, continuing Life as a potent factor in the cereal market.

In the long-term, companies such as Caterpillar, McDonalds, and IBM have staked out clear customer perceptions as "better" competitors. These firms could have spent too much or too little for advertising and promotion. They could have spent in less efficient, suboptimal media. However, execution of their positioning strategy was so successful that their advertising and promotion programs have worked over the long run—largely because of what they said, not how much they said, or where they said it. It cannot be emphasized too strongly how important up-front strategy, research, and positioning are to successful advertising and promotion programs. Nevertheless, management can even do more to increase the profitability of their advertising and promotion programs by improving the copy generation and evaluation process.

Management's Effect on the Copy Process

Figure 7-1 shows that marketing management can affect the structure of the creative process by choosing who will do the creating and how many different creative groups will work on the program. Management can also specify how the creative output is to be judged before it is actually executed. These copy testing decisions involve choosing the best testing methodology in terms of costs and benefits.

With top management's approval, many managers have implicitly given their full service agencies the authority over the above decisions on structuring the creative process. They use the agency's creative team and rely on the agency's expertise in copy testing and evaluation. As long as the output of the agency's creative process is acceptable and seems to fulfill the goals and objectives for the program, management is happy. Next, some arguments showing that the usual decisions being by advertisers and their agencies are not always productive as possible will be presented.

The creative process can be conceptualized as (1) generating creative copy alternatives and (2) picking one campaign to execute. Irwin Gross observed that it is better to choose from more creative copy alternatives than from fewer, particularly if the campaign alternatives are developed for free and the best copy alternative can be chosen.[1] In other words, it is better to choose among four alternatives than three as long as one can tell for sure which campaign will be most profitable. If the fourth campaign is not more profitable, then one of the first three will be used. If the fourth campaign is more profitable, then it would be used. However, creative campaign alternatives are not developed for free and, as we discuss below, it is difficult to forecast which campaign will work best.

Who decides how much to spend on developing creative campaign alternatives? If the full service advertising agency is compensated by a 15% commission, then there is an upper limit on how much the agency can spend on creative campaign generation and still remain profitable. According to Gross, the typical agency spends 20 to 33% of agency revenue—or the equivalent to 3 to 5% of a media budget—on creativity. The rest of the agency fee is used for media planning and buying, administration, and profit. The question that should be asked—and almost never is—is: Is this 3 to 5% spent on creativity in the best interest of the firm?

How Much To Spend on Creativity

Answering the question of how much to spend on creativity is neither simple, nor easy, nor precisely answerable. Other questions must be considered simultaneously: How much variability can be expected in the profitability of the campaign alternatives which would be generated if more money were to be spent? Is it possible to tell, *a priori*, if one campaign will do better (i.e., generate more profit) than another? Where should the most creative money be spent—on copy testing or on creativity? How should that decision be made? Which copy tests (if any) should be used?

Gross has developed a quantitative procedure and a paradigm to structure answers to the above questions. The quantitative procedure is too arcane to reproduce here, but the paradigm and conclusions have important management implications. Gross models management's control over the creative process in the following manner:

1. Management spends money to develop and test alternative campaigns. The campaigns that are developed have uncertain profitability implications. However, some alternatives are more profitable and others less profitable.
2. Management decides to generate a certain number of alternative creative campaigns.
3. Management also decides whether to assign the creation of each alternative creative campaign to different agencies or creative groups, different creative teams within the same agency, or the same creative team.
4. A copy test procedure is chosen by management and applied to each alternative.
5. The alternative with the highest copy test score is chosen to execute with the advertising and promotion budget.

Factors Influencing Copy Management

According to Gross's paradigm, there are five factors that should influence these copy management decisions. The first two factors are related to costs for each creative alternative and the copy test. How much would it cost for the creative groups that management has decided to use to prepare one alternative campaign ready for copy testing? How much would copy testing each alternative cost? These costs are interrelated. Some copy tests only need rough copy, while others require finished, produced advertisements or promotions ready for execution.

The next two factors—validity and reliability—are related to how good the chosen copy test is at differentiating among program alternatives. Validity refers to how well the test will predict the relative profitability of the alternative creative campaigns to be executed. Reliability refers to how stable test scores would be over repeated testing of the same program alternative.

The final factor in Gross's paradigm is the amount of profit variation there would be among the alternative creative campaigns if they were executed. The more profit variation there is among the alternatives, the more likely the best alternative will be more profitable. This concern with increasing variability is only because the paradigm involves deciding the best creative alternative to execute. For example, assume one creative group creates four campaigns, each having profit of about $5 million. Assume a second creative group also creates four campaigns, one having $0 profit, another with $2 million profit, a third with $8 million profit, and a fourth with $10 million profit. Both groups have the same average creative output of about $5 million profit, but the second group has more variability. Which creative group is best? If only one campaign is chosen at random from each creative group, on the average either group would generate a campaign of about $5 million profit. However, if the best of the four campaigns generated by each group could be chosen, the second group would be a better choice. Its best campaign is $10 million profit, while the first group is still at $5 million profit.

Gross's model concludes that in order to maximize the profitability of the creative process, one should have more alternative campaigns if:

1. They come from a process of higher profit variability.
2. Costs for creating each alternative campaign get lower.
3. Costs for pretesting each alternative get lower.
4. The copy test procedure achieves a higher validity level.
5. The copy test procedure achieves a higher reliability level.

Copy test validity and reliability are important because they govern how likely it is that the best (i.e., most profitable) creative campaign alternative will in fact be chosen. It doesn't help to have high variability in creative alternatives if management cannot choose the ones that will yield the highest profit if executed.

How Management Can Improve the Process

In general, management can improve the profitability of the copy generation process if it searches for ways to get higher variability in alternative creative campaigns and improve the validity and reliability of copy tests. What practical management alternatives are there to accomplish these goals?

How can management obtain higher variability in the profitability of alternative campaigns that are generated? Gross has done research to corroborate what common sense might dictate.[2] If more variability in creative output is desired, then creative input should be varied. If the same creative group is generating all of the campaign alternatives, then the profitability of these alternatives will likely be fairly similar. Even within the same agency, more variability can be obtained by having different creative groups within the agency work on the firm's account. If the agency has branch offices, different offices can supply creative groups with typically higher variability than groups from the same office. An alternative to an ongoing relationship with a single full service agency is to hire freelance, independent creative groups to develop alternative campaigns.

Interacting with Creative Groups

Not only can management strive for differences in the makeup of the creative groups; it can also encourage variability in the output by not overly constraining the creative groups. Management should provide guidance in objectives, strategy, roles, and positioning. Management should not prejudge which creative execution will best execute the positioning objectives. The now classic Avis "we try harder" campaign was generated by an agency, Doyle Dayne Bernbach, that was not constrained by management. Management should encourage their creative groups to develop alternative campaigns that they feel will be best given all the information available. They should also encourage the development of "different" campaigns because the more varied the alternatives are, the more likely one of them will be a real winner. Management should not prejudge which campaign style or tone would be best to execute the appropriate positioning objectives. Management should encourage development of campaigns of different styles for copy testing.

Gross described to this author how all Australian consumer products company's management successfully implemented these ideas on copy generation and tested them for their effect on sales and profits.[3] In the mid-1970s, the marketing director decided to test the idea of generating a number of independent alternative advertising campaigns before choosing one for ultimate use. At the time, the company had 13 brands that they regularly advertised among their extensive product line. In addition, they had two or three special advertising projects each year. These 15 or so activities had been divided among three advertising agencies.

For the test, the four most important and most heavily advertised brands were isolated. The remaining brands and projects were divided among four agencies (the three original, plus one added). They were to be handled in the usual way, with each agency given full responsibility for their assignments.

The agencies would, however, have to compete for the four

largest products. For the leading product, all four agencies were to submit proposals, including a 30-second commercial exemplifying each of their proposed campaigns. The other three major products were each assigned to two agencies for a similar competition. Hence, each agency had a one-in-four chance for the biggest product and a one-in-two chance for one or two of the three next biggest products. The agencies were promised a fee, intended to compensate them for about 90% of their expenses, for each of their losing submissions. The winners would, of course, get the accounts.

The instructions to the agencies were simple. Each was to deliver its proposals, including the commercials, by a given date. They had complete creative freedom. Any information they needed about the product or the market that the company had was freely accessible.

When all the submissions were in, marketing management judged them supported by copy test results, and chose a winner for each of the four products. There was almost universal agreement that virtually all the submissions were improvements over the previous campaign and the winners were major improvements.

This judgment appears to have been borne out by subsequent sales results. The unadvertised products experienced a slight sales decline relative to previous years. The advertised products, excluding the four brands competitively handled, showed a sales increase consistent with the trends of recent years. The four products for which competitive campaigns were generated showed a sharp increase in sales growth, despite the fact that these were the oldest and most well-established products in the line.

From the advertising agency point of view, competitions such as this one may cause increased management challenges. Constant creative runoffs may produce a poor creative atmosphere according to John Light who was an agency executive.[4] Light feels that the Australian example is not typical and that creative people do not do better jobs with "a gun to their head." Especially if management is not simultaneously improving the copy testing procedures (see below), this kind of competition can cause hard feelings and poor morale among an agency's creative group. Light's solution is to insist on different creative teams from the same agency. Some agencies may have different branch office creative groups working competitively on an account, for example. Light believes that good creative work and good campaigns require continuity between client company and the agency. His solution lets the client "have his cake and eat it too."

Copy Testing

Here is the big problem. All the management energy devoted to developing really different creative alternatives can be wasted if there is no effective way to pick the best campaign. The value of high validity and reliability of copy tests is obvious. If a copy test is going to be used to choose among a set of alternative creative campaigns, the cost of mistakenly choosing the campaign that is not the best alternative could be significant. For many products and services, shown above, the differences between good and average advertising and promotion campaigns can be millions of dollars in profit contribution. Valid and reliable copy tests are needed to distinguish between "good" and "average."

Most firms don't know—and are afraid to find out—how good their copy tests are. This is a strong accusation, but it is well-supported by facts.

Edward Tauber, currently at the University of Southern California and editor of *Journal of Advertising Research*, summarized the state of research on copy testing validity and reliability.[5]

In the realm of copy testing, we have long since ceased our search for truth. At a recent research conference session on recall versus persuasion, one speaker offered a litany of empirical support for why his opponent's method was invalid. He presented no evidence of the validity of his own position. The opponent simply appealed to social validity in defense—a majority of practitioners use the method. Hitler had social validity within the German nation, yet this is totally unsatisfactory evidence to support his actions in the context of most human value systems.

And herein lies our problem. Copy research has become religion—and often fanatic religion at that. Evidence is unnecessary when strongly held beliefs persist. On the contrary, facts are irrelevant, data would be shunned, proof is not expected. Can you conceive of "findings" that prove that Jesus did not exist or that there are five Gods or, worse, no God? If such unassailable truth were discovered, would followers of the world's religions make appropriate yet radical shifts in their positions? Of course not. We would *all* attack the data or the source or the assumptions. Rigid views are not easily reversed by evidence. If fact, we hope we are never faced with evidence. Isn't anything sacred?

When research methods become ideologies and dogma is widely professed, the search for truth ceases. Such a fate has befallen us in copy testing. And it is unacceptable. Scientific research is the antithesis of this type of religion. A researcher's role is to be inquisitive, objective, and challenging of conventional wisdom and ever seeking of truth. "Data support this hypothesis" is an acceptable researcher's response—not "I believe."

What should gravely trouble all of us is that data do exist, and we are ignoring them.

What can firms do to evaluate the reliability and validity of alternative copy testing methodologies? Reliability of a copy test can be evaluated by testing the same campaign more than once. If the retest scores of the same campaign are closer than the scores obtained when different campaigns are tested, then the test has high reliability. On the other hand, if there is as much variation in test scores when the same campaign is retested as when a different campaign is tested, the copy test is measuring nothing but sampling errors. It has no reliability.

Validity of a copy test is more difficult to measure. Validity measurement ultimately requires correlating the score achieved on the copy test with the profitability of the campaign in real world execution. Some companies could do this correlation by using different advertising or promotion campaigns in different markets and correlating their sales results with each campaign's copy test scores. The new instrumented test markets with split cable television which we fully discuss in Chapter 10 can also be used for validity testing of copy tests. In these markets, such as Information Resources' Behavior Scan, targeted households get different ads and their purchases are monitored unobtrusively.

A weaker test of copy test validity (called convergent validity) can be performed by testing the same campaigns with different copy tests. If a number of the copy tests all pick the same campaign as a winner, then some confidence might be placed in the validity of those tests.

An outsider observing the creation process for advertising and promotion campaigns would expect firms to be concerned about the validity and reliability of the copy tests that they use. Furthermore it is reasonable to expect that firms would find it valuable to undertake some of the above activities to determine reliability and validity of the tests they are using.

A survey by Ostlund, Clancy, and Sapra showed that most larger advertisers and their agencies are sticking their heads in the sand.[6] The survey covered a representative sample of 69 of the top 100 U.S. advertisers and top 100 advertising agencies. Over 80% of the responding advertisers and their agencies had no formal standards for assessing reliability or validity of different copy testing methods. Thus, the great majority of advertisers have the copy chosen for campaign execution based on testing systems that are not required to show any reliability or validity. Most testing methodologies were chosen because of availability of normative data by which to evaluate their test scores, the diagnostic ability associated with the technique, and the control provided over sample selection and test administration.

As long as the copy test was periodically able to pat the creative team on the back and say "you have done better than the norm" it was viewed as useful. Whether the "better than the norm" was due to luck (lack of reliability) or better profit potential of the campaign (validity) was rarely a consideration.

As discussed above, a firm can take relatively easy steps to assess the reliability of copy tests, that is, by testing the same campaign more than once with the same test. This reliability information is very valuable. A higher test reliability indicates a higher potential for truly choosing a more profitable campaign. More than half of the advertisers and agencies said that they test the same campaign twice with the same test less than 5% of the time. That statistic alone should cause one to question advertiser and agency rationality. Of even more importance, nothing was done even when inadequate reliability was found! The respondents were asked what action, if any, they took when a commercial tested two or more times by the same test produced significantly different scores (i.e., failed a reliability check). Only 13% of advertisers and 27% of agency respondents said they would reject the testing method because it was unreliable. Most advertisers and their agencies did not consider reliability testing as the reason for their retesting the same campaign. Only one-third of the respondents recognized that retesting a commercial using the same method gave them a check of reliability for the method.

There is a need to check reliability. The reliability of the most commonly used TV commercial copy test—day after recall—is somewhat suspect. In 1976, Clancy and Ostlund reviewed the published evidence on copy test reliability and validity. Their conclusion:[7]

> In summary, published data on the reliability and validity of alternative techniques for testing television commercials are in short supply. The data that do exist suggest that forced-exposure procedures may have greater reliability than on-air, natural-environment methods. Nothing is known about their relative validity as tools for measuring advertising effectiveness.

They then reviewed some proprietary tests by a major advertising agency of both on air, day after recall, and forced exposure. They concluded that the reliability of forced exposure tests was high but that "evidence has been presented that raises serious doubts concerning the reliability of typical on-air testing systems."

The large advertisers' and their agencies' actions, attitudes, and knowledge about validity testing of their copy testing were similar to those for reliability testing. Relatively few firms or agencies tested the same campaigns with different tests. If they did use different tests, it was almost always not to test for validity. Clancy, Ostlund, and Sapra concluded:[8]

> Thus with multiple testing by either the same method or by different methods, top U.S. advertisers and agencies do not display much deliberate interest in assessing for themselves the reliability and validity of TV-copy-testing methods.

By this time it might seem as though the search for a valid, reliable copy test is like the search for the holy grail! However, for a price, reliable tests are presently available. The scanner panels with split cable TV provided by such firms as Information Resources yield valid, fairly reliable copy tests. These firms use smaller towns that have only cable TV reaching them. They have the ability to control which commercials are exposed on the cable to different matched groups within the community. The exposed groups are also members of a panel that (for a rebate on their purchases) shows a card that is input into the Universal Product Code scanner computer at each store. These scanning computers thus unobtrusively keep track of purchases for the groups who are exposed to different advertising campaigns for a product. These split cable, scanner panel, copy tests can run to the low six figures to conduct depending on what other research on the brand is combined with the copy test. However, for many consumer products, where tens of millions are spent on advertising, such copy testing expenditures may be an excellent investment.

Fundamental Changes Needed

The arguments in this chapter have made a case for fundamental changes in the way management decisions are made that affect advertising and promotion copy. Copy is usually a more important decision than media or budget. Up-front decisions on advertising and promotion roles and objectives, market strategy, and positioning are all synergistic with effective copy generation. Top management should organize the advertising and promotion areas so that these areas can spend more on generating and testing highly varying creative program alternatives. Management should encourage variability in creative output by not overly constraining the creative teams, and using creative teams that are most likely to have different creative approaches. Chapter 9 discusses the organizational impact of these ideas.

Management must insist on consistent standards for reliability and validity of copy tests. Management should encourage spending money on evaluating the reliability and validity of alternative copy tests. The value of a proven valid and reliable copy test is very high.

In the copy area, just as in the media or budget area, the evaluation of the costs versus the value of research on copy testing is not being done explicitly. It is the chief executive officer's job to give someone with authority and suitable knowledge the task of determining profitable copy testing research budgets. This person should not have a personal stake in the decision from a short-term perspective. The individual should not be the research director who will get a bigger empire, nor should the person be the brand manager or marketing manager who doesn't have to account for the research budget. In most firms, the vice president for marketing should perform this cost versus value evaluation.

General Mills, Inc., one of the most effective marketers based upon long-term performance, is, coincidentally, concerned about developing more valid and reliable copy tests. Lawrence Gibson, director of marketing research, criticized agency researchers for not working toward more valid and reliable copy testing but instead continuing to "pander to their own creative departments by offering an emasculated research which promises help without discipline."[9]

Gibson reported that General Mills was continually working to develop validation evidence. His company evidently has realized the value of copy testing research: "We believe that decisions about advertising copy are very important, because the sales effectiveness of alternative ad copy varies enormously. Copy changes can reverse sales declines. Copy changes can cause sales declines."[10]

All of these management actions are needed simultaneously for increased profitability of the copy generating process. Finding reliable, valid copy tests is of no use if only one creative campaign is created. If more than one alternative is created, there is more variability among the creative options. Gross concluded, that if senior management revamped the advertising creative process so as to execute the above ideas, at least three times what is presently being spent on creativity and copy testing should be spent to maximize profits.[11] On the other hand, if firms continue to use only one creative source and continue to use copy tests of unknown (and questionable) reliability and validity, they are probably significantly overspending on creativity and copy testing!

Summary and Action Questions

- How important is copy to the firm's products and services?
- Has the firm's advertising and promotion campaign copy really been as effective as possible?
- Who in the firm decides on the make-up of the creative effort on the firm's products or services? Is anyone reviewing this decision periodically?
- Who is balancing the costs versus value of alternative copy tests in the firm? What criteria is being used? Which criteria are appropriate?
- What managerial steps can be taken to integrate the positioning research and strategic roles of advertising and promotion with the firm's copy-generating process?
- Has the firm attempted to measure the validity and reliability of its copy tests?

Further Readings

Special Copy-Testing Issue, *Journal of Advertising Research* (February-March 1982). Lots of food for thought here, especially Ed Tauber's editorial referenced below. Many articles evaluate methods of copy testing.

G.V. Ostle, and J.K. Ryans, "Techniques for Measuring Advertising Effectiveness," *Advertising Age* (June 1981), pp. 19–24. A much more qualitative review of some currently available copy testing procedures.

Notes

1. I. Gross, "The Creative Aspects of Advertising," *Sloan Management Review* (Fall 1972), pp. 83–109.
2. *Ibid.*
3. I. Gross, personal communication to author (1982).
4. John Light, personal communication to author (1983).
5. E. Tauber, "Shed the Faith Baby," *Journal of Advertising Research* (February 1982), p. 9.
6. L. Ostlund, K. Clancy, and R. Sapra, "Inertia in Copy Research, *Journal of Advertising Research* (March 1980), pp. 42–48.
7. K. Clancy and L. Ostlund, "Commercial Effectiveness Measures," *Journal of Advertising Research* (February 16, 1976), pp. 29–34.
8. See Note 6, *supra.*
9. L. Gibson quoted in "Copy Testing Flap Continues," *Marketing News* (May 15, 1981), p. 7.
10. See Note 9, *supra.*
11. See Note 1, *supra.*

❖ 8 ❖

Media Decisions

Media planning is concerned with answering the following two questions: Which media should be used? When and how often should ads be placed in these media? This chapter assumes that a budget has already been determined and that a copy strategy has been determined for each alternative media type that we can consider. The chapter discusses how the media plan affects the budget and the copy strategy. The effect depends on whether more or less efficient media can be found or on whether there is an interaction between the copy strategy and the chosen media. Senior management should be aware of what goes into making decisions about the media, for example,

- Who really cares about media decisions?
- Who should care about media decisions?
- What role should the CEO and senior management play in media decisions?
- What are precisely wrong rules of thumb for evaluating media plans?
- What are vaguely right approaches for media plan development and evaluation?
- What is the role of media research and experimentation?

As in the budgeting chapter, there is a tendency here to develop precisely wrong rules of thumb for media decisions. In many instances, media planning decisions are not really being carefully considered. Strong top management leadership is needed to design incentives for and center action toward vaguely right media approaches. This chapter begins with a discussion of the present extent of decision support for media planning. It next discusses the concepts and issues necessary for a vaguely right media planning process. The chapter concludes with steps top management can take to improve the decision-making process.

Who Really Cares About Media Decisions?

More than $65 billion was spent in the United States alone on media by advertisers in 1982. Given that level of expenditure, it is quite disconcerting to an outside observer that few people really care about where that money is spent. Who should care? The obvious answer is the firm who is paying for the advertising. However, marketing managers feel that the answer is the advertising agency. For some companies that are doing à la carte advertising, the answer is that the media buying service should be concerned.

Agency Motivations

But do all advertising agencies really care about media planning? Let's look at their motivations:

- Advertising agencies make profits by gaining new accounts and keeping them for a long time.
- They lose profits when they lose accounts.
- Few advertising agencies have gained or lost business because of good or poor media planning services.

As discussed in Chapter 7 on copy decisions, copy is usually much more important than media planning in the priorities of advertising and promotion decision making. Most advertising agencies gain or lose business because of their perceived creative excellence. Some agencies tend to view media planning as a necessary evil to be contended with in order to fulfill their obligations to the advertiser. "Media is tedia" is a slogan one sometimes hears in advertising agencies. The high salary, high visibility positions in most advertising agencies are in the account service and creative areas—not in the media planning or media buying areas. The sterotypical media person is a young, recent college graduate, who majored in English and wants to get into advertising. The media department route is the only way for such a person. However, it is difficult to get a job in a creative department because the positions are so important.

It is less profitable for advertising agencies to buy some media types rather than others. It almost costs as much administratively for the agency to purchase a national $150,000 television spot as it does to buy a $50 local radio spot, for example. An advertising agency makes more money if it puts an advertising budget into national media, such as television or magazines, which are less costly to buy into than local media or media that must be bought in small chunks. What is more profitable or less costly for the agency may not be in the advertiser's best interest, however. As will be discussed in Chapter 9, it probably pays for the advertiser to directly compensate the agency for its administrative costs and for processing media buys. In this way, both the advertiser and the agency will have the same motivations.

Agency Presentations

Some advertising agency presentations of new advertising campaigns underscore their lack of concern for effective media planning. A scenario for a presentation might go like this: The agency account executive first describes in detail the marketing strategy and positioning that underlie the advertising campaign. Next, a discussion of copy alternatives and copy strategies is covered with an extensive behavioral and marketing rationale for the execution that has been chosen. Then the advertisements or the commercials are shown to the advertiser. Finally, a media plan is presented along with a budget. The budget recommendation is carefully documented. The media plan is shown with bar charts summarizing where and when the media will be placed. A thick book full of statistics about the potential exposures of the media plan to various important market segments accompanies the charts.

Alternatives Are Missing

What is almost always missing from the media plan is explicit consideration of the affect on sales of alternatives. The thick book of media figures is quite complex and full of media jargon such as gross rating points, average frequency, net reach, etc. The aura is given of careful attention to detail. However, attention to detail in media planning is usually related to precisely wrong objectives that are easily evaluated by computer. As shown later in this chapter, media planning is like budgeting: It is better to be vaguely right rather than precisely wrong.

There is one group that is always concerned about media planning decisions—the media themselves. Media gain or lose sales and profits based on the media planning decisions of advertisers and their agencies. Most of the research in media is supported by the media, not by the companies or advertising agencies the research is really valuable for. For example, A. C. Nielsen, Simmons, and Media Mark, the three largest syndicated media audience surveys, are supported mainly by the media—not the advertisers and their agencies.

Just as advertising agencies spend top dollar to get effective account executives, media spend top dollar to get effective sales people. Thus, there are a number of situations of highly paid, highly skilled media sales representatives calling on lower paid media planners and advertising agency buyers. There are all kinds of possibilities for irrationality in this mismatch of people.

What can top executives do to improve this state of affairs? CEOs can provide direction, motivation, and incentives for their people to care! They can ask questions about media planning.

More important, CEOs should make sure that the top marketing officer in charge of accepting media plans rejects any plans that don't consider and rationally evaluate alternative media planning decisions. This tactic will cause the company's advertising people to direct their agencies or media buying services to treat the media planning problem more carefully. Top executives also need to provide an organizational environment that promotes media research that is valuable to decision making in relation to its cost. In order to ask questions and provide appropriate incentives, the CEO should be familiar with the jargon and some of the basic concepts and issues of rational media planning.

Concepts and Issues in Media Planning

The important issues in media planning can be illustrated by a discussion of alternative methodologies for solving the media planning problem. Any media planning methodology—be it quantitative, qualitative, or "seat of the pants"—either explicitly or implicitly has three parts: (1) generating alternative media plans; (2) developing an evaluation model (either a complex, mathematical computer model or a qualitative one) that either explicitly or implicitly relates an alternative media plan to some measure or number describing how good that plan is; and (3) finding an implicit or explicit method, be it simple or computer-based, for choosing the best media plan from all the feasible options.

As in making copy decisions, generating alternative media plans may be more important in the process than the evaluation or choice steps. The firms that first thought about advertising on Chinese laundry shirt cardboards or putting plastic bread wrappers on the delivered morning newspaper found cost-efficient ways of reaching their target markets. Adidas made a profit by putting its name on T-shirts it sold. Weren't the first designer label jeans part of someone's creative media plan? Creativity in media can sometimes be as effective as creativity in copy.

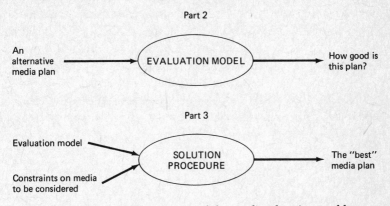

Figure 8-1. The conceptual parts of the media planning problem.

In evaluating the alternative plans, the reviewer must know how the plans differ. As shown in Figure 8-2, alternative media plans deliver different numbers of exposures to different people from different media at different times. Thus, the evaluation of alternative media plans can be further broken down into two parts. The first part includes questions such as where are exposures going from the media plan? To which people? From which media? At which point in time? The second part compares how good that distribution of exposures is in relation to other media plans.

Conceptually, the first part of the evaluation is relatively straightforward. Needed information includes identifying the media audience, that is, who is reading, watching, or listening to which media. The media audience is broken down by market segments of interest to the advertiser. Generally, the information is gotten from syndicated surveys of individual media habits. In order to calculate whether exposures are all going to a small group of people or are being distributed among a wider group, it is important to identify how the media audiences of different media overlap.

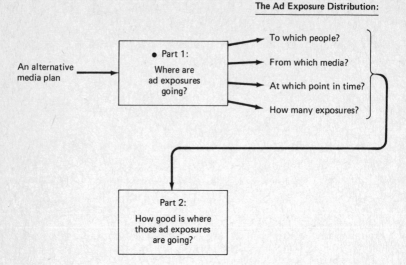

Figure 8-2. Two conceptual parts of a media evaluation model.

However, it is not enough to just know that exposures are potentially going to a particular media audience. We must also know whether people are actually being exposed to the specific product ad that was placed in the vehicle. For example, knowing that someone reads *Iron Age* magazine is not enough. What fraction of the people that are counted as reading *Iron Age* magazine will see the one-page color ad about the product? Similarly, of those people who are counted by Nielsen as being in the audience of a television show, what fraction of them will actually be in front of the TV set watching a particular commercial when it comes on? Media audience numbers need to be reduced to reflect the probability of exposure of an audience member to the particular ad type that the firm is planning. In other words, how much of the media audience is actually comprised of the important market segments as determined by the firm's initial, up-front marketing strategy and product positioning. Over the past 15 years, computer programs that do a suitable job of taking a media plan and counting to whom and how many times the exposures are being generated have been developed. The big problem is evaluating whether the exposure distribution from schedule A is better than the exposure distribution from schedule B.

The precisely wrong approach to evaluating media plans is to just count potential exposures. For television, this means adding up the rating points of each of the commercials utilized in a schedule. A rating point is defined as the percent of total homes or of a market segment that is tuned in to the particular commercial. This is termed the gross rating points of the campaign. For print vehicles, a similar calculation involves adding up the total ratings of advertisements that are placed in magazines or newspapers. The ratings here are the percent of the target audience that is counted by a readership survey as reading the particular vehicle. This is typically known as the audience of a schedule. If the total audience of a schedule is divided into the cost of a schedule, the cost per thousand audience members of the schedule is determined. Many media planners and media buyers prefer to judge the effectiveness of their media planning and buying by how low their cost per thousand audience or cost per gross rating point is above alternative media schedules. In almost every case this is a precisely wrong methodology (see Table 8-1).

There are a number of other factors that affect how people respond to advertising. These factors may be different for alternative media schedules having the same gross rating points or audience. What are some of these factors?

First, the relative worth of different market segments must be considered. Is an exposure or a set of exposures to a person who is a heavy user of the product the same as the value of an exposure to someone who is a heavy user of a competitor's product? It is this decision on relative worth of market segments that integrates media planning with earlier decisions on product positioning and market segmentation. Exciting new data that links TV viewing with product usage is being generated as

Table 8-1.   Why Are Gross Rating Points, Reach and
Average Frequency, or Cost per Thousand Audience Usually
Precisely Wrong?

STATIC CONSIDERATIONS	• Relative worth of different segments • Potential versus actual ad exposure • Ad exposure from different media may have different effect, for example: 1. TV vs. print vs. radio 2. Color vs. black and white, 1 page vs. ½ page 3. Different environments for the exposures
DYNAMIC CONSIDERATIONS	• When are exposures made to individuals? • How often are exposures made to individuals? • What is the market response to different exposure distributions? • Over what time period are we calculating response? • Memory and forgetting

a by-product of the UPC scanner panels and instrumented cable TV markets described in Chapter 7.

Second, just because a person is counted by a survey as being in the audience of a vehicle does not mean that any particular ad has been seen. It is very hard to measure the fraction of a media's audience who are exposed to a particular ad. Yet it is the exposure to the ad—not exposure to the media in which the ad appears—that causes the advertising to work.

Third, do exposures from different media have the same effect? Depending on the product or service being advertised and the creative strategy employed, there may be large differences between the exposure effectiveness of different media classes. A TV ad may have a different effect from a print or radio ad. Not only may the media class have a different effect, the different characteristics of the advertisement within the option may have a bearing (color vs. black and white, 60 second vs. 30 second, etc.). The environment in which the ad appears may also have a significant effect on the reader or viewer. For example, is there a difference in a potential customer seeing our ad in

Business Week or *Time* magazine? Again here our product positioning is an important consideration.

This media environment affect might be caused by a number of factors. These include the attitudes of the media audience toward the media, and the perceived unbiasedness, expertness, or prestige of the media. Also important may be the mood which the media promotes or the degree of involvement of the media audience member.

The foregoing factors are all relatively static considerations. Complicating matters is the fact that there may be a large difference in response in media schedules depending on when and how often the exposures are received by individuals in the target audiences. The precisely wrong approach to exposure distribution is to consider only the reach and frequency of the media schedule. The reach of a schedule is simply the number of people potentially exposed to one or more of the vehicles in the media schedule (i.e., an unduplicated audience). Frequency is defined as the average number of potential exposures the audience received from the media schedule. Gross rating points (which are essentially the total potential exposures delivered by a schedule) can be obtained as the product of the reach times the average frequency.

Reach and frequency are not enough to evaluate alternative media plans. Two media schedules both with an average frequency of five and a reach of 70% of the population may have different effects on the target audience. One schedule may have almost all of the population seeing exactly five exposures; another could have some of the people seeing many exposures and many people seeing only one or two. Computer programs are available to determine this distribution of the number of people being exposed potentially once, twice, three times, etc. It's the evaluation of how superior five exposures are to four exposures that becomes imprecise, although it is still important.

The timing of an exposure is an even more complex issue. Reach and frequency calculations are usually done over a 13-

week period. It is clear, however, that there may be widely differing effects of media schedules that have the same reach and frequency but that are calculated over different time periods. An interesting question to ask media planners is why they have chosen the period that they have for their reach and frequency calculations.

Timing of exposures has to do with such things as memory and forgetting, seasonality, and the response of target segment populations to repeated exposures. It is beyond the scope of this book to go into detail on each of these phenomena. They all have been shown to one degree or another to affect the sales of alternative media plans. For more details on these phenomena, a good description is found in Aaker and Myers, *Advertising Management*.

When a media planner has chosen one alternative media schedule over another one, an implicit decision has been made about all of these vaguely right factors. A vaguely right approach that explicitly attacks these phenomena will usually cause significant changes in media schedules. An example of an experience the author had recently illustrates this problem.

A Vaguely Right Example

A regional bank had one-half million dollars as a budget for savings account advertising for one year. Two people at the bank were ultimately responsible for the advertising decisions. These people were the advertising manager and the vice president of marketing to whom the advertising manager reported. They had both been in their same jobs for the past five years. The marketing vice president had routinely approved the advertising plan submitted by the advertising manager each of those years. The advertising agency had been on the account for the past 10 years. The vice president of marketing decided to use MEDIAC, a complex dynamic media model[1] to take a more analytical look at his media planning. As part of the implementation of that model the explicit evaluation of some of the vaguely right factors discussed above were performed.

The first problem was determining which market segments were more important to the firm in terms of advertising responsiveness. If the bank's objectives were to increase current savings account deposits for that year, some segmentation by income would probably have been desirable. If, however, the bank's objective was to maximize the long-term amount that would be put into savings accounts, the emphasis of their advertising could be shifted to younger people who would have money in the future even if they didn't have it now. It took one-half day of discussions between agency people and the two bank representatives to develop an age-income segmentation that attempted to consider both long-term and short-term objectives. This long-term versus short-term problem had never come up before because there had been no explicit consideration of segment importances in the media planning process.

The determination of the appropriateness of alternative media types was an even bigger problem for the team. There were many options that were used in the past and many others that were available for possible use. These ran the gamut from outdoor advertising to radio to regional editions of magazines and newspapers. Arbitrarily, a one-half page ad in a local newspaper was set as average. Each member of the decision-making team made their own independent evaluations of the media-segment appropriateness weight for each of the 25 media options under consideration. An example of the evaluation decision that they needed to make for each option was as follows: "If it costs me $1 to have a person in this segment see my ad in the one-half page newspaper option, how much more or less than $1 am I willing to spend to have that same person hear my ad instead on a 60-second radio spot or see a 30-second television spot?"

The interesting outcome of these estimates was the fact that the two people from the agency were at least in relative agreement as to the order of the media-segment appropriateness weights for different media types, that is, print, broadcast, radio, or outdoor. However, the advertising manager and the vice president for marketing at the bank were both diametrically opposite in every one of their estimates of media-segment appropriateness weights. If the vice president thought that regional magazines were more valuable than the local paper, the advertising manager thought just the opposite. Yet, they had been routinely approving each other's plans for the past five years!

In the ensuing discussions, each person on the team talked about their estimates and described phenomena that they considered important in making them. The rest of the team members learned a lot about the assumptions that had been implicit in everybody's media plans for the past five years, but had never been made explicit before. It took one full day of discussion to develop a consensus set of media-segment appropriateness weights for this particular problem. In the final solution, certain radio stations and some local newspapers were clearly ahead of all the other media options. In the past the bank had spread out its budget over many media options, from outdoor through broadcast. However, after rationally evaluating all alternatives, the team realized that they should spend all of their money in the top two ranking media types.

Since there was no test group that was not exposed to the media plan, it was difficult for the bank to determine whether the media plan that they ended up with for that year was better in terms of its objectives than those of previous years. However, both the rate of growth and market share of savings accounts did increase slightly that year. The team that was involved in making the decision felt, however, that they had done a much better job of media planning that year than prior years because they explicitly analyzed the important assumptions that needed to be made in order to evaluate alternative plans. In the past, their predictive model and their solution procedure had been nonexistent.

The Role of Media Research and Experimentation

Media research and experimentation can prove valuable in improving the sales effectiveness of media plans by giving more

	City	Regular Newspaper	TV	Magazines	Radio	Extra Newspaper
Control	Detroit Houston	(X X)	xNov Dec		xOct Dec	
TV	Jacksonville Phoenix	(X X)	(X X)			
Magazine	Minneapolis Philadelphia	(X X)	xNov Dec	(X X)		
Radio	Salt Lake City Milwaukee	(X X)	xDec xDec		(X X)	
Extra Newspapers	Denver Tampa	(X X)	xDec			(X X)

Circled usages are designed; the rest were not.

Figure 8-3. The media experiment—design and execution.

precise answers to questions that defy facile evaluation. The two examples discussed below illustrate this value.

A Media Experiment

A large retailer with many stores was trying to determine the best media to advertise a successful 2-year-old consumer electronic product. The advertising agency was recommending and primarily using, magazines and some newspaper. Other people in the company were recommending extra newspaper, radio, and television. A experimental design was developed where two cities each received one, and only one, media used aside from normal newspaper for three months. Figure 8-3 shows the experimental design. The circles indicate what was supposed to have happened. Notice, however, that there was some slippage when some of the markets found out that there was television available and used it in some of the months. Other markets used radio when they found out it was available. The central

Table 8-2.   National Implications of the Experimental Results

Media	Estimated Sales per Thousand Dollar Media Expenditure	Lower Bound on Estimate	Upper Bound on Estimate
Newspaper	$ 7,252	$3,516	$10,987
TV	$11,741	$8,732	$14,750
Radio	$ 7,170	−$3,072	$17,412
Magazines	$ 4,200	−$2,741	$11,140

people who were monitoring the experiment did not know of the additional media usage until after it was done.

Data for the product was captured on electronic cash registers, and the results were available within a week after the experiment was finished. What the advertising agency did was simply to total up the sales during the experiment compared to sales before the experiment for each of the treatments. They then concluded that magazines were the best media alternative. An analyst working with this author, however, realized that there could be many factors aside from the media treatment that would cause the results that the agency found. The analyst figured that the size of the cities might make it more likely for the product to succeed since the magazines happened to be the experimental media in the largest cities in the study. The analyst then performed a careful statistical analysis using multivariate procedures to isolate the effects of both population and the situations where the experiment was not followed carefully. The effects of jointly having TV and radio or TV and magazines in some of the markets for some of the months were then factored out statistically.

The analyst's conclusions are reproduced as Table 8-2. Notice that the statistical precision on these estimates shows that television was much more profitable than magazines. In fact, magazines might not have been more profitable than no advertising at all.

The results of this experiment completely changed the media

plan from using magazines heavily to one using television heavily. The advertising budget for this product was $5 million. How valuable was this experiment when it showed that productivity of the advertising could be increased by a factor of two or three? How much was this experiment worth? It was worth a lot more than it cost. Even if this experiment cost a half a million dollars—or even $1 million—it would have been worthwhile. How many companies even think of spending that much money for a media experiment?

Color vs. Black and White

The second experiment was valuable because it showed a firm how important color advertising was versus black and white, compared to pricing and promotion. A retailer used an experiment to simultaneously determine regular price level, sale price levels (price break percents), and media characteristics (color versus black and white newspaper ads) for a new fashion-oriented home furnishing product. The test design is shown in Table 8-3.

Table 8-3. Experimental Design: Objective—Determine Best Combination of Price Level, Price Break, and Advertising Color

| | TEST SCHEDULE | | |
| Primary Price Points | Promotion Schedule | | |
	Price Break (%)	Advertising	Markets
Normal—$30	10	B/W	Kansas City
	20	B/W	Buffalo
	10	Color	Sacramento
	20	Color	San Francisco
Medium—$35	15	B/W	San Diego
	25	Color	Portland
High—$40	15	Color	Spokane
	25	B/W	Seattle
Control—$30	0	B/W	Dallas
	0	Color	Tampa

Table 8-4. Experimental Results

	Mean Units Sold per Million $ Store Sales
Price Point (regular sales)	
$30	.0000030
$35	.0000035
$40	.0000025
Price Event Sales	
10% off	.0000018
15% off	.0000011
20% off	.0000018
25% off	.0000017
Advertising During Price Event	
Color	.000022
Black & White	.0000098

The results of the experiment showed management that consumer sales were the same for both the high and low prices and for the different levels of price break percentage. However, the color advertising of a price event was extremely productive. These results are summarized in Table 8-4.

Note that the color advertising doubled sales levels compared to black and white. This difference was statistically significant while the other experimental variables showed no significant differences in their sales effects. These results were quite unexpected. Management's interpretation was that it was important to the consumer that the item's colors would look nice in their homes. If it did, then the item was seen as a reasonable value, even at a $40 price. However, sales were much higher in all markets during the price events when the items were temporarily reduced. All the advertising was done during the price events. Evidently, a temporary price reduction (no matter whether the reduction was 10% or 25%) was a powerful sales stimulant.

Both of these experiments were valuable to the firms that

performed them. However, they were also costly relative to customary media research. As an investment, the value of the information in terms of the increase in sales that resulted from decisions that were made was an excellent return. As in the budgeting process, the top executive must create an environment and an organization in which a rational evaluation of the cost versus the value of media research and experimentation is carefully considered.

The Media Future

Some forces are combining to cause media decisions and media planners to become more and more important to the advertiser in the future. Media technology is creating new media. "Media is growing and growing in importance," said Page Thompson, senior vice president and director of media planning at Needham, Harper & Steers. "We have cable now, we're going to have satellites in five years, every house is going to have a disc. You have to be aware of it. The star of media is going to be very bright in the '80s."[2]

But with the technological turmoil comes a multitude of new challenges and problems: "What are we going to do about cassettes?" Mr. Thompson asked. "What about the disc? You can't put a commercial on a disc because people will just skip ahead. Maybe you put it in a wraparound or cover. There has to be a new way of doing things," Mr. Thompson said. "We have to find them."[3]

The new media create new opportunities for programs directed toward specific target segments. Some advertisers and their agencies may be back in the programming business. Needham, for example, has its own programmer, Bill Cameron, senior vice president in charge of programming, on the West Coast looking for cable programs—primarily variety, cultural, and talk shows, according to Mr. Thompson. Mr. Thompson made this comment about his agency's cable programming activities: "We have been on the road with our clients for over a year, giving them an idea what's happening in the marketplace, what the implications are," said Mr. Thompson. "One of those implications is programming. Programming is going to make or break cable."[4]

However, even with all the new electronic media and new programming options, the basic media planning problem still remains: Which media should be used? When and how often should ads be placed in them? The vaguely right concepts supported by appropriate research, testing, and experimentation are just as appropriate for the future media alternatives as those of the past. Strong top management leadership is and will be needed to design incentives for and center action toward more rational media planning.

Summary and Action Questions

- Who is making the firm's media planning decisions? Are they motivated to consider all the vaguely right concepts discussed in this chapter?
- Who is balancing the costs and benefits of media research and experimentation? Is that person able to make that decision in order to maximize the long-term sales and profitability of the product or service?
- How does the media planning decision relate to upfront decisions on positioning and segmentation?
- Why aren't gross rating point, reach, and frequency suitable by themselves for evaluating media plans? What other factors are needed?
- Who are media salespeople in charge of the firm's media plans? What is their influence on the media planning process? Can it be improved?

Further Readings

D. Aaker, and J. Myers *Advertising Management* (Englewood Cliffs, N.J.: Prentice-Hall, 1982). The best available textbook on advertising; its approach is scientific and rational. A great place to find more references for most advertising problems.

D. Gensch, "Media Factors; A Review Article," *Journal of Marketing Re-*

search (1977). A review of all the different ways media may be different in their effectiveness.

R.I. Haley, "Sales Effects of Media Weight," *Journal of Advertising Research* (June 1978), pp. 9–18. Nice methodology for media weight tests using experimentation.

Notes

1. J. Little and L. Lodish, "A Media Planning Calculus," *Operations Research* (Jan.-Feb. 1969), pp. 1–32.
2. C. Marshall, "Agency Media Executives Coping with Change," *Advertising Age* (March 23, 1981), p. 10.
3. See Note 2, *supra.*
4. See Note 2, *supra.*

❖ 9 ❖

How To Get and Keep Effective Advertising and Promotion Services

No senior executive is going to write creative copy, implement promotional programs, evaluate alternative media environments for advertising the firm's products or services, develop effective brochures or trade show exhibits, and so forth. It is the CEO's job, however, to make sure that the process that is used to generate advertising and promotion does produce the most effective advertising and promotion possible given the resources of the firm. The firm's resources involve more than money. They also involve the skills of employees or suppliers who are involved in advertising and promotion decisions. Therefore, choosing the right advertising and promotion services is difficult:

- What are the advantages and disadvantages of alternative methods for obtaining advertising and promotion services?
- What are the strengths and weaknesses of alternative compensation methods for outside services?
- When should suppliers be changed?
- How should new suppliers be evaluated?

Executives would agree that one of their most important decisions is hiring and firing personnel. If one has excellent people to work with, it is relatively easy to plan strategy and execute procedures to implement the strategy effectively. If the employees are only mediocre, the manager must devote a lot of time solving problems that would not have occurred if only excellent people were employed in the manager's group. Not only must the effective executives recruit and retain good people, they must also motivate them to make and implement decisions that accord with the goals and objectives for the firm. Hiring good people and suppliers and motivating them effectively are also critical to advertising and promotion decisions. Senior management could accept all the recommendations contained in this book, invest all the time and attention necessary to monitor the advertising and promotion programs, and still not obtain effective advertising and promotional programs.

This chapter evaluates concepts and methods for obtaining effective advertising and promotion services. The structure of alternative methods for obtaining advertising and promotion services and conceptually evaluating the advantages and disadvantages of each will be considered first. The discussion will move on to implementation, where the focus will be on such issues as selecting and/or changing advertising and promotion services and designing compensational incentive systems to motivate advertising and promotion professionals. These concepts will be related to the common industrial and consumer marketing practice of retaining full service advertising and promotion agencies. These agencies are typically compensated on a commission basis, although sometimes a fee is paid.

Make, Lease, or Buy?

Some of the concepts involved in structuring advertising and promotion services are analogous to those involved in making, buying, or leasing machinery. What are the critical considerations in determining whether to develop internally, buy, or lease advertising and promotion services? Certainly economies of scale figure prominently here. Advertising production is a high fixed cost operation. Television advertising production entails much expense and requires considerable technical expertise. It is a rare company that could even consider internal production of television commercials. Similarly, large sweepstakes or consumer promotions entail large fixed costs for certificate and coupon redemption mechanisms, and so on.

However, there are other aspects of scale economies in advertising and promotion services that might not be as obvious. For example, effective buying and planning of media involves knowing media alternatives and learning about their audience environments, among other things. This learning is a fixed cost which in some cases may be spread over many clients by an advertising agency or media buying service. Similarly, as the prices of some media are negotiated (i.e., television, radio, and some print vehicles), the development of good negotiating contacts is also a fixed cost that may be spread over many clients. However, if the firm is in a specialized market with specialized media, it might be more appropriate to do the media planning and buying in-house because the firm's employees may be better able to negotiate with the specialized media. This may be especially true in industrial or highly specialized consumer markets. For example, a firm that produces components for industrial robotics and is infinitely familiar with media of that idustry would probably be able to make better decisions as to which media are most appropriate for its advertising than the great majority of advertising agencies or media buying services. Similarly, on the consumer side, a company that makes bicycle components for racing bikes would probably be most familiar with which media would reach bicycle racers and stores specializing in bicycle racing.

When one buys or leases outside advertising and promotion services, an important feature of these services is the cumulative experience of the people providing them. In some cases this can be very valuable. For example, any kind of direct marketing experience with products or services similar to your own can be extremely helpful. Knowing what works and what doesn't work in terms of improving the draw of direct response campaigns can save many dollars spent on experiments. It is useful, for example, to know whether a personal note or an impersonal form letter is required to maximize response to a campaign. Do consumers in your target market respond better to contests and sweepstakes designed to induce them to buy products or services or is a more refined approach more appropriate? For example, Revere Chemical, a chemical firm selling roofing supplies to industrial and commercial customers has successfully used sweepstakes to get the attention of industrial buyers for years. Their advertising agency has a great deal of experience in helping other companies who might want to sell other kinds of maintenance products to the same audience using direct response methods because they would know what works and doesn't work.

Other kinds of experience can also be helpful when obtained from outsiders. Techniques such as barter have become increasingly important to many firms as means of obtaining advertising and promotion services at attractive prices. However, if a firm is not experienced in developing barter arrangements, they can end up shortchanged. Barter is another area where economies of scale come into play. Some of the large barter houses are able to capitalize on large inventories of barter goods to effect more advantageous transactions for each of their clients. In many cases, it is worth the fee of the barter house to have access to many more firms with which to barter goods and services. Sometimes the barter house even provides these goods and services by performing the service of holding those bartered items in inventory.

Obtaining Quality Services

Aside from economies of scale and experience, the quality of advertising and promotion services varies depending on whether they are made, bought, or leased. As seen in Chapter 7, creative copy that effectively positions and sells the product or service can be worth a fortune. Compared to the media buying or planning decision or the advertising budgeting decision, the copy platform and its execution is usually the most leveraged in terms of the advertising or promotion effect on most firms' sales and profits. Thus, one benchmark that is required in determining the structure of advertising and promotion services is how these services affect the likelihood of obtaining the creative advertising and promotions that really make a difference in terms of the sales and profits.

These are at least three ways of obtaining creative services. The first is to hire an internal creative team or person who does all of the copy platform and execution determination for the products or services. Good creative people who have demonstrated effectiveness in developing successful advertising are usually quite expensive. In terms of economies of scale, only the largest firms could think about affording an in-house creative group that would be busy just developing advertising for the firms' products or services. Also, many creative people like working on different kinds of problems and they might find themselves stilted by continually focusing on a limited number of products or services. If the product or service is technical and so specialized that an outside creative person would have to spend months learning about the business in order to be able to write copy, however, it might be appropriate to have an in-house creative team.

Most firms obtain outside creative services from full service advertising agencies or a creative boutique (i.e., a freelance group that specializes in the creative function). Each of these external sources has advantages and disadvantages. The typical full service advertising agency probably pays its creative people better than a creative boutique does. This is because the creative people at some full service advertising agencies are leveraged by the agency's media percentage fees and production overrides.

What works creatively is quite variable. It changes from time to time as the marketplace and competitive conditions change. Commitments to full service advertising agencies are relatively long term, however, and are generally viewed as partnerships. The creative approach of one full service agency may not be appropriate for changing times, though, and problems can arise.

Sometimes a firm makes a long-term commitment to obtain effective creative services from a full service agency and only get a short-term gain. On the other hand, creative boutiques and freelancers may not, on average, be as effective creatively as those people in a full service agency. However, since the client is buying them on a shorter-term, more flexible basis, the client can use more of the boutiques or freelancers and therefore increase the amounts spent on creative compared to media. This flexibility, which is difficult to achieve with most full service advertising agency relationships, helps increase the variability of creative sources. Also, it is much easier to change creative boutiques and freelancers than it is to change full service advertising agencies. Thus, if one sees that the creativity is not producing advertising that is successfully performing the required role, one can easily change the creative boutique that is working on the account.

Rational Measurement Is Important

There is no one way of structuring advertising and promotional services that will fit every firm. Aside from qualitative considerations of economies of scale, experience, and possible creative outputs, knowing whether the present system is effective is an important part of the process. The CEO who insists on rationally measuring the effectiveness of advertising and promotional programs will know whether the structure of the advertising and promotional services is working. All of these structural decisions are based on balancing increased effectiveness of advertising and promotion to the costs of the various services, be they produced in-house, purchased externally, or leased. Management that doesn't know the incremental effect of different advertising and promotion services will find it difficult to make these evaluations. Thus, the CEO can implement steps to make the firm a better buyer of advertising and promotion services.

Alternative Structures for Media Planning and Buying

As discussed in the media chapter, with some exception, some standard full service advertising agencies have little incentive to spend time or money evaluating alternative media and planning alternative media schedules. In-house agencies or the company itself can also do media planning. There are fewer economies of scale in the media planning area than in other areas of advertising and promotion decision making. To reiterate, the decisions that need to be made in media planning involve the correct environment for advertising, evaluating the audience overlaps, and the reach and frequency of alternative media schedules. There are a number of external syndicated services having computers that do an adequate job of the number crunching involved in media planning. The judgments on appropriate editorial and other environmental variables can probably best be made by people who know the market, competition, and, above all, their potential customer. This person is typically an experienced, in-house marketer. However, a lot of coordination must exist between the media planners and the creative people with the appropriate vehicles. Thus, the coordination between creative and media planning is probably better done in a full service agency, but the planning by itself could probably be done more efficiently in an in-house agency or by the company.

Media buying—as opposed to media planning—offers many potential economies of scale and experience. For those media in which prices are negotiated, having a larger amount of advertising to place makes the advertising buyer a more effective negotiator. Thus, there is an advantage for large media buying services and advertising agencies in this process. Also, as discussed above, having good contacts and knowing intimately the people who are selling the media probably facilitates better negotiations on media buys. The secret of using outside media buying services effectively is to give them precise instructions on what to buy. It is important to measure the output of the media buying services in terms of the ratings or audiences of the vehicles in the precise market segments that were outlined by the media plan. If specific guidelines are not set up, the media buying services may end up buying what is easier to negotiate rather than what is in the firms' best interest.

Structures for Industrial Markets

The advantages and disadvantages of different structures for media and creative are slightly different for industrial marketing than consumer marketing. The advantages and disadvantages of each were nicely outlined by Gary Lewis, then Manager of Advertising and Publications of Steelcase, Inc., who concluded "if your media changes vary little from year to year and you feel your inside people know the subject, you may not need an agency to select and place it for you."[1] Lewis also mentions media evaluation services and suggests that "perhaps you will need this service only once every couple of years, or when your targets or markets change."

The creative trade-off for industrial products is different from that for consumer products. According to Lewis, "the costs of keeping top-notch talent at an agency mean that you are going to have to pay for it. Most creative types will tell you that their consumer accounts allow for more exciting and creative approaches than the comparatively dull industrial stuff. None of us believe that, but the creative young copy writer may well opt for the consumer rather than the industrial account."

"The result, frequent changes in the copywriter on your account. This means frequent retraining and rewriting the copy submitted. The option, of course, is to have it done by an outside creative group, who will charge you only for that job on an hourly basis." Lewis also notes that the area of technical and sales literature can be a problem for a full service advertising agency. Typically, the same person who does the creative advertising does the technical and sales literature. However, the creative person usually finds this fairly dull, and either delays doing it or does it without giving it optimum concentration. Furthermore, an agency creative type may not have the skills. Technical writing is a skill in its own right. Lewis recommends specialized firms that do little else other than technical literature, direct mail, or audio visual material:

> There the assignment for a technical brochure may go to an engineer who will gather information and write it. Direct mail preparation and list selection may go to a specialist who does nothing else. Your audio visual project may go to the same production house that the agency may have used minus the markup. The timing and budget control are the strong suits of these specialists.

Lewis' comments are probably just as appropriate for many technically oriented consumer products that need lots of brochures and sales literature.

Structure Trade-offs

Thus, for both consumer and industrial marketers, there are many options open for structuring advertising and promotion services. The biggest advantage provided by standard full service advertising agencies is a coordinated approach to all the firms' advertising (and sometimes promotion) problems. They also will have higher paid creative people because of their leverage by other services, other accounts, and commission arrangments. At the other extreme is the in-house agency, which may minimize the out-of-pocket expense for advertising and promotion services. In the middle is the à la carte or cafeteria structure that gets specialists to independently help with specific parts of the problem. The à la carte approach offers more flexibility in spending compared to media planning and is easier to change. Table 9-1 summarizes the attributes of each type structure.

Not all firms need the same structure. Over time, the appro-

Table 9-1.   Some Factors To Be Evaluated in Choosing Structures for Advertising and Promotion Services

Full Service Agencies

ADVANTAGES	DISADVANTAGES
Coordinated approach of media, copy, positioning, etc.	Harder to change the relationship
Higher paid creative people	Higher in cost
Stability of relationship	Less attention paid to specialized collateral material
Negotiating clout with media	Difficult to get widely variable creative options
Experience with similar products or markets	
Advertising research	

In-house Agencies

ADVANTAGES	DISADVANTAGES
Lower out-of-pocket costs	Harder to retain top flight creative people
More control	Less experience with similar products and services
Easier coordination with marketing strategy	Less negotiating clout
Can pay more attention to specialized collateral material	Difficulty to get widely variable creative options
	Harder to change the relationship
	Less independence of recommendations

À la Carte Cafeteria Style

ADVANTAGES	DISADVANTAGES
More flexible relationships	More difficult to coordinate media, creative, and positioning
Easier to get widely variable creative options	Lower paid creative people
Can pay more attention to specialized collateral material	True administrative costs may be hidden because more coordination is needed
Possibly lower out-of-pocket costs	
Possibly more negotiating clout over media	

priate structure may change. How many companies periodically audit how well their structure is working and evaluate alternatives? Some firms periodically review their advertising agency, but few will, as a matter of policy, question the basic structure of the methods they use for obtaining advertising and promotion services. All the normal pressures on marketing personnel push them toward the structural status quo. Only alternatives that are deemed to be within "corporate policy" are usually considered. If there has always been an in-house agency, then considering a full service agency would be difficult to do without top management support. Similarly, if the firm has always dealt with full service agencies, other alternatives will usually not be evaluated. Only top management can create the climate and policies that encourage marketing management to periodically evaluate the suitability of the structure for the particular time and circumstances. Making such periodic structural evaluations happen is one important job of senior management.

Compensation for Outside Advertising and Promotion Services

The problem of determining appropriate compensation methods for advertising and promotion agencies is conceptually similar to that of compensating outside salespeople. Each party (the company and the salespeople) has objectives which are always not congruent. However, top management has paid much more attention to the generation and evaluation of alternative salesforce compensation schemes than to advertising or promotion agency compensation. In most firms, historical precedent dictated the methods of agency payment. This section shows that the two historical methods of 15% commission and fixed fee are probably not the best methods for most firms. Some more suitable alternatives will be suggested. Here again, only top management can initiate discussion of new alternatives.

The definition of reasonable objectives for agency compensation depends on which side you are on—the company's or the agency's. Colantone and Drury summarized these possibly conflicting objectives.[2] They are enumerated in Table 9-2.

Table 9-2. Compensation Objectives

Advertiser	Agency
1. Value must be received for the money spent.	1. Sufficient income must be provided to cover costs and provide a profit.
2. Costs must be predictable and controllable.	2. Continuity and predictability of income should be assured.
3. Charges must be easy to verify.	3. Billings must be simple to calculate and verify accurately.
4. An atmosphere must be provided for unbiased recommendations and efficient purchasing.	4. Agency must be permitted to maintain control of its management perogatives.
5. Agencies should have incentive to use time efficiently.	5. Client should have incentive to utilize agency's time efficiently.

Source: R. Calantone and D. Drury, "Advertising Agency Compensation: A Model for Incentive and Control," *Management Science* (July 1979).

Evaluating the Standard Commission

Given the objectives, how does the standard 15% commission basis stack up? As Colantone and Drury observe, "There can be rigid administration and financial control on both sides. The advertiser can predict and control his costs while the agency can easily prepare and verify the billing. However, note that the compensation technique is based on inputs and, consequently, there is no direct relationship with the outputs or services provided to the advertiser." Over the longer term, there may be a relationship between the value of the agency's output and its income because successful products usually enjoy larger advertising budgets.

Some biases may be inherent in the commission system. The most commonly discussed bias is that of agencies toward recommending higher budgets that result in higher fees. There are two other possible biases of the commission system that have been observed but not frequently discussed. The first bias is toward low buying cost media. The second is toward optimism for new products.

Under the normal commission system, the agency is compensated exactly the same no matter which media are bought.

As pointed out in the media chapter, if some media involve higher administrative costs to purchase the same dollar amount, then the agency will find it less profitable to purchase them, even if the higher administrative cost media are more appropriate for the client. For example, the agency's administrative costs to buy a one minute TV spot for $150,000 are not 1500 times as high as buying one local radio commercial for $150. All things being equal, national TV campaigns are much less costly for the agency to administer than a series of local radio campaigns of the same cost. When the Wells Rich Green advertising agency was still a public company, securities analysts commented that the agency was profitable because it concentrated on large national accounts whose media budgets were largely devoted to national TV with relatively low buying costs.

An advertising agency has many fixed costs in developing a campaign. The commission payment encourages the agency to try to spread those fixed development costs over a larger media budget. In new product situations, this possible bias can be quite pronounced. If an advertising agency has developed a campaign to use in a test market for a new product, the agency will typically only make a profit on the campaign if the product is deemed successful in test and introduced nationally. It may be difficult for the agency to interpret negative test market results realistically in such situations.

The Fixed Fee Compensation System

The other compensation alternative that has been tried is a negotiated overall fixed fee or a fee based upon agency outputs or services. According to Colantone and Drury, this system also has advantages and disadvantages:[3]

> This method has the advantage that it can meet administrative objectives on both sides. There are not time consuming verification problems. Unfortunately, because it is based on outputs, there is no incentive for efficient agency buying and unbiased recommendations. Also, often the client does not use the agency's full potential and services properly and this causes much time consumption. Finally, the method is again based on predetermined

measures of services. If the situation changes or the agency fails to estimate properly, it can over or under charge the client. Either result can have serious consequences.

Some firms have tried results-oriented compensation systems where the agency is paid according to results such as sales, share, or preference rating changes. This system is no cure-all, either.

It is obviously dependent upon the contribution the agency makes to help the client. But it is a time unrelated technique that is almost entirely to the client's advantage and the agency's disadvantage. The agency might not have enough income to cover costs and income can no longer be predicted accurately. Also, if the advertising (or promotion) is not the major marketing variable, then the agency's compensation is based on an unrealistic measure which is unrelated to the inputs required.[4]

The current trends in agency compensation are away from commissions and toward fees. However, commissions are still the most common payment method. According to a Association of National Advertisers, Inc. survey,[5] 52% of firms used a form of media commission system in 1982. This is down from 57% in 1979 and 68% in 1976. In 1983, 29% of firms used some sort of fee-based system.

All the current compensation schemes have two basic problems involving the firm's expectations of agency results. It is in the agency's best interest to convince the firm that any expectations or targeted results per unit of agency input should be low. On the other hand, over time an agency will not be lured to overfill a current low results target because the next year's—which is based on the current year's success—target may be set too high. The agency and the firm need to generate reasonable expectations to coordinate other elements of the production and marketing processes.

A Different Compensation Approach

Calantone and Drury recommend a three-stage approach to agency compensation. This plan tries to minimize the problems exhibited by each of the current systems.[6] In the first stage, the agency assigns a fair target output value measure (e.g., sales, share, or preference) and a tentative compensation level to the firm. The advertiser then chooses a planning incremental payment for each unit by which the target output value measure is either exceeded or unfulfilled. In the second stage, the agency is given the option of selecting a different planning target (either smaller or larger) with a larger or smaller payment based on the planning incremental value. Finally, in the third stage, the firm determines a system of penalties and bonuses by which the agency will be compensated if it misses or exceeds the agreed on planning target output value.

The appropriateness of this approach depends on the particular firms' objectives. However, the process of generating alternative compensation schemes and evaluating them in terms of the effect on both the firm's and the agency's motivations and objectives is a worthwhile approach. Such an approach does not develop spontaneously. Senior management must ensure that it happens periodically, especially when relevant objectives are changed. If the CEO diverted 10% of the effort that is usually expended on salesforce compensation to compensation alternatives for advertising and promotion, the firms' long-term sales and profits would probably increase.

Changing Advertising and Promotion Services

Deciding when advertising and promotion suppliers should be changed is not easy. Theoretically, the answer is simple: when the value of changing is greater than the costs. In practice, the decision is very difficult. The value of changing is always relative to the current services. How likely is it that a new agency or supplier will provide advertising or promotion that will be better (i.e., more profitable) than those currently being supplied? If a manager knew for certain that a certain supplier would provide better service, the change would be straightforward. However, there are costs associated with finding out how much "better" an alternative supplier might be. For example, many advertising and promotion agencies are charging fees for speculative presentations. In order to evaluate these alternative speculative programs, some costly research is also needed. Other costs for changing suppliers may be even more expensive, for example:

1. The executive time spent on the search for alternative suppliers.
2. Meeting and communication time of marketing executives to exchange information with the new agency or supplier and establish new relationships.
3. If supplier changes are too frequent, the firm may get a reputation for lack of loyalty. (Conversely, if one never changes suppliers, the firms' business may be taken for granted.)

As discussed in Chapter 7, it is usually worthwhile to attempt to get more than one alternative creative source for big leveraged advertising and promotion programs—provided reasonably valid and reliable copy testing research is available to pick the best alternative. The firm whose managers are following the rational approach recommended in this book will have more information to make these trade-offs. If management is continually testing, experimenting, and monitoring the effectiveness of their advertising and promotion programs, they will have a good picture of their current status. They will know if advertising and promotion are continuing to perform their appropriate roles in the marketing mix. The decision to change suppliers will always be based on judgements of known versus unknown quantities. The more that is known about the effectiveness of the current supplier's work, the less uncertainty there is about at least one of the alternatives—that is, the status quo.

Evaluating New Suppliers

The basic purpose of evaluating new suppliers is to estimate their potential incremental value to the organization. Any information that can be used to increase the precision of the measurement of that potential value increases the likelihood of making a more profitable decision. However, such information may be costly. Should one pay for creation and evaluation of speculative presentations of potential campaigns? The copy chapter says yes in many highly leveraged instances. One can supplement that judgment by other criteria:

1. How good is the track record of the people who will be creating the advertising and promotion programs for the firm's account?
2. What is the attitude of the people who will be working on the firm's account toward rationality and unbiased evaluation of their efforts?
3. What kind of compensation plan will they work with?
4. How receptive are they to new methods for generating and evaluating alternative approaches to their area of expertise?
5. How adaptive is this proposed relationship to changing circumstances, for example, relationships with full service agencies are more difficult to change than those with independent creative boutiques or media buying services.
6. Finally, do the firm's people and the agency's people communicate effectively?

If advertising and promotion are important elements in the firm's marketing mix, then it may be worthwhile for the CEO to be directly involved with major decisions on changing the structure, compensation, or the identity of advertising or promotion suppliers. If the CEO is not personally involved, only he or she can create the managerial environment and objectives so that these decisions are rationally considered. Having the best players who are motivated effectively makes the coach's job a lot easier.

Summary and Action Questions

- What incentives can the CEO provide to encourage periodic evaluations of the structure of the firm's advertising and promotion services?
- What are economies of scale in advertising and promotion in the firm's

business? Does the firm's advertising and promotion service structure take advantage of them?
- What appropriate ways are there for the firm to generate creative alternatives for its advertising and promotion?
- How are the firm's advertising and promotion services compensated? How does it compare to other alternatives discussed in the chapter?
- Does the firm change suppliers too often? What are the trade-offs involved in making such changes?

Further Readings

R. Calantone, and D. Drury "Advertising Agency Compensation: A Model for Incentive and Control," *Management Science* (July 1979), pp. 632–642.

Association of National Advertisers, Inc. *Compensation Survey*. New York, N.Y.: Association of National Advertisers, Inc., 1983. The current status of various agency compensation methods.

Notes

1. Gary Lewis, "In House vs. Full Service Agency," *Industrial Marketing* (June 1979), pp. 68–72.
2. R. Calantone, and D. Drury, "Advertising Agency Compensation: A Model for Incentive and Control," *Management Science* (July 1979), pp. 632–642.
3. *Ibid.*
4. *Ibid.*
5. "The 15% Media Commission is on the Way Toward Becoming a Relic," *Marketing News* (June 10, 1983), p. 9.
6. See Note 2, *supra.*

❖ 10 ❖

Decision Support Systems for Advertising and Promotion

This book recommends a rational, no nonsense approach to all advertising and promotion decisions and the marketing strategy decisions that must precede them. These decisions should be supported by the best information and judgments available. It is, therefore, important to know the answers to these questions:

- How can the profitability of advertising and promotion decisions be increased by improving the associated decision support system?
- Why is market response reporting more valuable to top management than market status reporting?
- What are "naturally occurring experiments" and why are they valuable to management?
- How can decision support systems be misused?
- How should management evaluate research, tests, or experiments? What is the cost versus the value of such information?
- Who in the organization should control a marketing decision support system?

Why is the concluding substantive chapter of this book on decision support for advertising and promotion? This area is one where CEOs and senior executives have the most leverage for affecting improvement in both the long- and short-term profitability of advertising and promotion decisions. Senior management does not need a book like this to identify and foster qualities such as creativity, leadership, guts, and follow through in marketing management. What is needed is more astue, insightful, scientific methods applied to marketing. Modern Decision Support Systems (DSS) for marketing are the bases for:

1. Generating more advertising and promotion alternatives.
2. Evaluating more alternatives more carefully.
3. Choosing better alternatives.
4. Controlling the decision's implementation.
5. Balancing the trade-offs between costs now and profitability in the future—that is, balancing the costs and value of information.

Decision support for planning and evaluating alternative advertising and promotion decisions generates predictions of sales and profits realized under different action alternatives. Effective decision making in an advertising and promotion context requires predictions of what would happen if different media were used, different budgets were allocated, different promotions were offered, different positionings or strategies were taken up, and/or different copies were employed. For control purposes, once a program has been implemented, management is also interested in what did happen and how it compared to the prediction that was made.

Market Status vs. Market Response

Useful information to support advertising and promotion decision making is quite different from the kind of information that most firms currently compile. Most firms gather data on what is currently happening in the marketplace? This kind of information is useful for financial reporting and external evaluations of the firm and its products and services. However, market status information is of little use for improving advertising and promotion decisions. To improve advertising and promotion decisions, information for "what would happen if" scenarios is needed. That is, how would the market respond to changes in the firm's advertising and promotion decisions? If the firm is

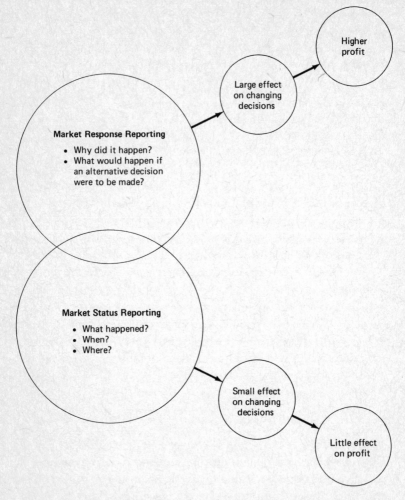

Figure 10-1. The value of market information.

only aware of how a current advertising and promotion program is doing, it will lack the requisite information to improve the program by changing other decision factors.

Information is valuable to managers only when that information may alter management decisions. If it merely causes management to continue doing what they would have done in the absence of information, then the information has no value in terms of its contribution to the firm's profitability. Most market status information doesn't change management decisions and isn't supposed to. Typically, it is not valuable. Management will only change its decisions when the market status information indicates that a program is not working. Thus, if market status reporting shows insufficient market response to a particular program the information has some value. However, there are many circumstances wherein management may be unaware that other programs could be much more profitable than the current one. Unless information about the sales and profit response of alternative programs is made available, management will not make these better decisions. Progressive senior executives should encourage their marketing organizations to allocate more resources to market response reporting and less resources to market status reporting.

Information for Decision Support

Information for market response can come from two basic sources: (1) naturally occurring experiments and (2) planned experiments and tests. Planned experiments or tests are designed to measure or predict the response to changes in advertising and promotion variables. Naturally occurring experiments are situations where, for other reasons, advertising and promotion variables have been changed at one place or one time, but not changed generally. In some cases, analysis of naturally occurring experiments can be a fruitful source of information about market response to changes in advertising and promotion variables. However, the analysis of such situations has to be done with great care, given the lack of controls and normal experimental procedures. In general, planned experiments require the same analysis as naturally occurring ones. However, the analysis for naturally occurring experiments is typically more difficult because one has to factor out all the uncontrolled variables statistically. These variables are typically controlled in a designed experiment.

For example, The PROMOTER Decision Support Systems, codified from 15 years of experience by Magid Ibrahim and the author, supports improved trade promotion decisions by analyzing naturally occurring experiments in trade promotions over time and different regions.[1] The PROMOTER DSS provides managers with four beneficial functions:

1. *Evaluating* past trade promotions to determine their sales and profitability impacts compared to no promotion.
2. *Diagnosing* the reasons for differences in sales and profit effectiveness among the promotions that were evaluated.
3. *Recommending* more profitable future trade promotion actions.
4. *Tracking* and control of future trade promotions by comparing predicted sales and profits due to the promotion to actuals. This is an early warning system for possible problems.

All of the above functions are provided without gathering any new data for most companies. The new DSS technology enables an analyst to statistically isolate the aspects of normal sales and shipments data from naturally occurring experiments that have implications for market response rather than market status. Good model building and statistical analysis also enables assessment of the risk associated with alternative decisions. Figure 10-2, for example, shows the probability of losing money for each district by increasing the average trade promotion allowance by 1% for the 15-ounce size of a consumer household product. Only in three districts is there a high probability of this being a wrong decision. Before firms were using a DSS like PROMOTER, they had little hope of systematically improving their trade promotion effectiveness.

Decision Support System Elements

The full value of most naturally occurring or planned experiments is seldom realized. This failing typically stems from deficiencies in one or more elements of the decision support sys-

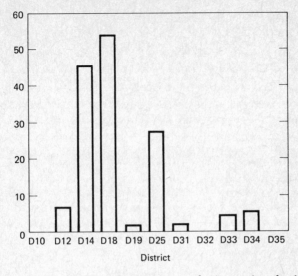

Figure 10-2. Probability of losing money by increasing the 15 oz. trade discount by 1%.

tem required for effective analysis. Such elements include data, models, statistics, computers, and an interface person.

In order to analyze either naturally occurring or planned experiments, it is necessary to know what was done and what happened. It is amazing how many companies do not even maintain their own data, let alone analyze it for the results of naturally occurring experiments. These firms do not realize that aggregate data that is useful for summarizing market status is not useful for analyzing naturally occurring experiments. Naturally occurring experiments sometimes occur at disaggregate levels, such as different regions, cities, or accounts. If the data on sales at the disaggregate level are not preserved, then it is no longer possible to analyze naturally occurring experiments. Therefore, it is crtical to know both the sales data and the marketing variables associated with those sales. Again, it is amazing how many companies don't keep unambiguous records of what advertising was run at any particular point in time at a disaggregate level. However, companies often know when advertising was paid for because their accounting records show that.

Other data makes analysis of naturally occurring experiments even easier. Many other factors—such as environmental data, weather, economic trends, and so forth—may contribute to the response to an advertising or promotional program. It is useful, therefore, to keep track of such information. It is also worthwhile to maintain information on competitive activity in as disaggregated a form as possible. Competitors often have a large impact on the response to programs. In many cases, the firm's salespeople are a good source of competitive information. If this information is not routinely catalogued, it will not be available for explaining anomalies in naturally occurring experiments.

Preserving the data is not enough; the data must be transformed into information that is useful for decision making. Isolating this information requires mathematical models and statistical analysis. Uncovering the true response when there are many other factors that might cause changes is the primary statistical and model building challenge for the analyst and the computer. Even with the most expert statistical analysis, one can never be sure that the naturally occurring experiment is providing an unbiased answer on sales response to advertising and promotion variables. The best that statistical analysis and model building can do is generate hypotheses regarding possible actions that seem to result from marketing activities. Depending on the relative importance of the output of this analysis, it may be useful to develop formal or planned experiments, or market research, to validate the hypotheses that are generated by this historical analysis of naturally occurring experiments.

Even with excellent data, model building, and statistical analysis, the output from naturally occurring experiments may still not result in profitable actions unless the appropriate manager understands what transpired and receives answers in time to affect decisions. There has to be easy access to the models, data, and statistics so that the analyst can perform his work in time to affect decisions. If a decision is needed next week and the computer analysis will be done three weeks from now, it might as well not be done at all. Not only must the analysis be timely, it must be in a form that management can understand. Thus the computer system that is used must have easy access to the graphs, charts, and reporting procedures that enable the output of analysis to be intelligible to management. This access to intelligible output should be combined with the flexible statistical and modelling capability for a truly productive computer based decision support system. This computer technology is now readily available. However, its availability may be a mixed blessing.

Possible Problems with Decision Support Systems

There is a tendency in marketing (as well as in other areas) for computers to be used to make people's jobs easier rather than better. Managers have a tendency to concentrate on the use of computers to eliminate clerical labor and automate the drudgery parts of management jobs. However, the real potential of the new decision support technology is to make better advertising and promotion decisions. Since most "hand done" clerical procedures used to analyze marketing data were fairly simple, some managers are gravitating toward simple computer-prepared marketing analyses.

There is great potential for misuse of automated, simple analyses of naturally occurring experiments. For example, there has been a growing usage of menu-driven, computer systems. These computer systems have menus of reports that management may choose at their option. Because the menu is limited, there is a limit to how complicated an analysis can be. Most menu-driven systems look at data two or three factors at a time. They use cross-tabulation or various plots of marketing instruments, such as advertising or promotion and sales over time.

These systems are wonderful for hypothesis generation. That is, developing questions that need thorough answers. However, without both appropriate checks and the interpretation of a knowledgeable analyst, these reports may cause more harm than good.

Nevertheless, it is difficult to resist a beautiful graph relating advertising and sales in a multi-color format. A disturbing trend is apparent in management's attraction to pretty pictures that are generally the result of unsophisticated and not necessarily valid analyses. GIGO—garbage in, garbage out—was a true description of the data processing that was popular 10 or 15 years ago. There is a new slogan that has just become popular and is even more true today: Garbage in—color garbage out."

What can management do to minimize some of these dangers and simultaneously take advantage of the large potential of this new decision support technology? At present, the computer terminal and monitor is not the best interface between a somewhat naive management and the new technology. Just because the new technology makes it easy to sit down at the computer terminal, it doesn't mean that the results that come out will be perfectly correct or implementable. Significant, productive changes in management decisions have been made when interface people were employed to be the liaison between the manager and the new technology.

The Role of Interface People

The interface people have two very important skills: They understand the business and the strategic problems that firm management faces and they also understand enough about data analysis, statistical analysis, and modelling to make sure that the appropriate checks and questions have been asked when a recommendation based on computer analysis is made. These interface people should be reporting directly to top and middle management and matrixed with a staff group to control the quality of the analysis that is being performed. It is important to insure that at some point the analysis the manager is using to make a important strategic decision has been reviewed carefully by someone who understands what data analysis is about.

Eventually, this group of interface people won't be necessary. Artificial intelligence research will some day enable the computer to do as careful a market response analysis as a good analyst would do. The computer will imitate what the best analyst or interface people have done. That day has not arrived, however.

An implication of this need for interface people is that MBA programs at analytical business schools are even more valuable to management. They will be a source for interface people. These schools are targeted toward management problems and analytical support for those management problems. All of them have good courses on marketing research, data analysis, and information systems. The position of an interface person can be a perfect entry level management position for an ambitious MBA, once he or she has spent the required time to learn the business.

The example of the media experiment of TV, radio, magazines and newspaper done for the consumer electronic product in Chapter 8 illustrates this point. The simple, straightforward, aggregate analysis of sales broken out by planned media treatment was shown to be erroneous. The careful analysis of the data that simultaneously considered city size and the actual versus planned media treatments on a monthly level gave different conclusions. If the firm had gone with the simple, incorrect analysis and used magazines instead of TV, the advertising would have been less than half as productive. The technology just isn't here yet to do a complete, careful, market response analysis automatically.

Designing Market Tests

There is as much art and common sense required in designing planned experiments and market tests as there is in analyzing the naturally occurring historical experiments. Planned experiments can have different degrees of reality and different causal factors associated with them depending on the objectives of the tests. It is often appropriate to use survey research to estimate sales response to marketing variables. For example, positioning is typically done with survey research. Sometimes the use of simulated laboratories may be appropriate. These tests have people brought into a laboratory-type environment, exposed to different elements of an advertising, promotion, or marketing program, and then observed in terms of their reaction. Successful results can often be obtained if careful attention is paid to making laboratory environments as realistic as possible, and unrealistic aspects are statistically factored out. For example, for frequently purchased consumer products, a simulated test market environment can predict the share of the market that a new product will receive a year after it is produced.

In other cases, actual in-market tests are necessary in order to measure the elements of the advertising or marketing promotion program. Here, the experimental units can either be geographical or, in the case of split cable TV, the experimenting units can be defined by how the cable reaches each family. Another method of in-market experimentation that isn't used as much as it should be is split run of magazines and newspapers. For a fee, most magazines and newspapers will put different advertisements in different editions.

Joseph E. Seagrams & Sons, Inc. and Time Inc. conducted a very successful in-market experiment utilizing split runs in *Time* and *Sports Illustrated* to subscribers in Milwaukee and the state of Missouri.[2] The test ran for 48 weeks in which different people in the study were exposed to different numbers of ads for eight Seagram liquor brands. Some people received copies of the magazines with no ads for a given brand, some received copies with one ad each month, some received copies with two ads per month, and some received four ads. Smaller groups of the test population were interviewed each week about their brand purchases, awareness, advertising recall, and attitudes.

The findings of the study were of obvious value to the Seagram company as a source for improved profitability of their advertising decision making. One of the authors summarized some of the important findings this way:

First, advertising does enhance consumer awareness, favorable attitudes, and use and purchase of a brand. Generally, too, the greater the advertising pressure, the better the results. And—this was a surprise—for the most part, gains were still being achieved after 48 weeks of these campaigns.

We found large initial effects—the first ad did produce, in most cases, large gains. It appears that even a little advertising has an effect after a prolonged period of no advertising. We found that low awareness brands showed greater attitudinal effects due to advertising than high awareness ones. (It may be that even though some brands have high awareness, they have been rejected on the basis of experience. That is, attitudes and impressions do exist for high awareness brands, and they may be so entrenched that it may be easier to change behavior—'I'll try it again'—than it is to shake people of attitudes and impressions created by previous experiences. Perhaps for low awareness brands—and this includes new brands—consumer attitudes are more susceptible to learning from advertising.)

How should management evaluate planned research, tests, or experiments? The goal is to do experiments, tests, or research when the profitability resulting from decisions that are likely to be changed as a result of the tests is greater than the research costs. If decisions won't be changed as a result of the research, it shouldn't be done. The usual market status reporting is not that valuable because, in most cases, it does not cause decisions to be changed—and, therefore, does not affect the profitability of the firm.

Much of the advertising and promotion research that might be construed as market response reporting rather than market status reporting is not helpful for improving decision profitability either. The research does not relate alternative decisions to firm goals such as sales and/or profits. Most of it involves measuring intervening variables such as recall, awareness, attitudes, and so on. The advertising and promotion objectives chapter, Chapter 5, discusses this in detail. The relationship of intervening variables to sales and profits must be estimated as part of the research or testing.

Consider consumer coupons, for example. Most firms look at redemption rates of coupons as a measure of their success. What has this to do with profit? The key question is what would happen if a different promotion were run or if the coupon promotions weren't done at all. The advent of scanner panels has permitted the precise measurement of the incremental profitability of coupons. The scanner panel is a group of people in a city who are given an identification card that they use whenever they shop at stores that have scanners in them. As an inducement to use the card, they are granted a percent rebate on all purchases that they make where the card is shown. These scanner panels get large response rates and are unobtrusive, longitudinal measures of consumer purchases over time. They are usually done in cities where most or all of the stores are equipped with scanners. The Management Decision Systems Metric Coupon Laboratory, a syndicated service, mails out different coupons to one group in a scanner panel and no coupons to a matched control group.[3] They then get unobtrusive sales measurements longitudinally over time of groups that have been exposed to the coupons and groups that have not. Figure 10-3 shows the sales effect of two coupons. It's quite easy to measure those incremental sales compared to no coupon. Notice that before the arrow in the figure the coupons had not been mailed. Their sales effect is obvious.

The figures only show the short-term, evident sales effects of the coupon drop. In order to determine the extent of long-term effects, mathematical models of consumer brand choice and loyalty must be applied to see if there has been any changes. Do those who get coupons have a long-term change in loyalty? Is the use of a coupon for an established product by somebody who had not tried it for a while just like a new trial for a new product? Most managers who use coupon promotion justify their use partly on that basis.

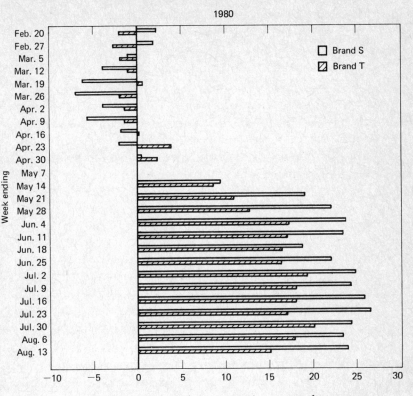

Figure 10-3. Cumulative test minus control.

The syndicated coupon lab has a decision support system associated with it to do this long- and short-term analysis. The service also follows through, not just with sales, but also with the profitability of the coupon drop. (See Table 10-1.) Note that the comparison here is incremental profitability versus not doing the coupon drop. This is a reasonable, realistic way to calculate profitability. Note, too, that there is a large loss per thousand for every coupon sent out.

Most coupons seem to get only short-term share changes without long-term effects. It seems as though coupons for established products are mostly used by people who randomly switch purchases depending on whose coupon they have. Thus,

Table 10-1.   Profitability Calculations
(per Thousand Coupons)

	Brand A
Incremental purchases (Effect of × Weeks × Penetration)	85.8
Average purchase price	$ 1.20
Retail margin	20%
Factory gross margin	40%
Incremental gross margin per unit	$ .384
Incremental gross margin per thousand coupons	$32.95
Distribution costs	$14.00
Redemption rate	12.3%
Redemption cost per coupon	$ .44
Couponing cost	$68.12
Profit (loss) per thousand coupons	($35.17)

the coupons do not seem to change long-term loyalties in most cases.[4] However, most brand managers are reluctant to stop couponing for mature, established products because they fear their share will decline. It is a valid concern—their share will decline. However, profits will increase in many cases. Unfortunately, most brand managers are judged on sales rather than profitability.

Are there differences in management decision support systems for advertising and promotions because of industrial, services, or consumer product efforts? Not really. All the concepts discussed in this chapter are appropriate for all types of products. Only the data will be different. The same criteria are needed to evaluate decision support systems and the same reasons for success in supporting decisions will apply to a service or an industrial products firm. The Bell Telephone Company of Pennsylvania has both industrial and consumer advertising campaigns aimed at convincing both industrial companies and consumers to utilize long distance for more of their communication needs. Although the data is different and the economic variables that influence consumer versus industrial long distance calling are different, the statistical analysis and the mathematical model that Bell of Pennsylvania uses for evaluating naturally occuring advertising experiments is conceptually identical for both consumer and industrial advertising campaigns.

Suggestions for DSS Improvement

How can top management improve decision support systems for advertising and promotion? First, they can encourage their managers to spend as much for creative analysts and interface people as for good general managers. Second, management must listen to these specialists. It is a rare person who understands the firm's business and understands the research, experimentation, and computer procedures that are needed to support truly profitability decisions. If they are heeded and well-supported, such people can be extremely effective in improving sales and profits.

The marketing decision support system should be controlled by the marketing department reporting to the marketing vice president. It's really an extension of market research. Market research should control their own computing resources. The technology of mini- and micro-computers along with much improved and more powerful software have enabled the interface people directly to build and maintain decision support systems. Trends indicate that this type of end-user computing, with the decision maker controlling the computing to support his or her decisions, will become widespread by 1990.

The goals of decision support system computing contrast with those of the data processing departments. The data processing departments are rewarded for computing efficiently. This is a small side consideration of the decision support system. Computing for decision support is aimed at improving the profitability of decisions. DSS computing needs qualities such as flexibility, modularity, multidimensionality, ease of use, interactive access, easy graphs, charts and reports, and easy customization. These contrast with the basic attributes of data processing systems: repetitive, cheap, efficient, and so forth. If the marketing department does not control its decision support systems resources, then most DSS applications end up lower in priority than payroll, accounts receivable, and other accounting applications that data processing shops typically manage. These accounting procedures, because they are time dependent, always seem to drive out the other applications on a large main frame computer.

Central data processing should be a first-line collector of corporate sales data and other data. This data, which is useful for decision support, should periodically be fed to the marketing DSS for interpretation, analysis, and model building. As decision support systems proliferate for other areas of the firm besides marketing, such as strategic planning, each of these groups will have their own computing source. The data processing department will become more and more a data collection and disbursement agency rather than a data processing agency.

An even bigger issue in decision support for advertising and promotion decisions is balancing the cost versus the value of decision support system information. As seen throughout this book, the value of most information is long term whereas the cost for collecting and interpreting it are short term. In most organizations these costs are not explicitly balanced. Most corporations are overspending on research that is not related to decision profitability such as market status reporting. They are underspending on truly valuable market response reporting research. Throughout this book suggestions were made for how to improve this balancing procedure. One way is to put directly into management by objective programs the requirement that each manager spend some money or perform actions during this year so that the person who is running the operation in the following years is able to better understand the response of the market to the advertising and promotion decisions that are made. Another possibility is to give product and marketing managers profit responsibility for products—not just sales responsibility. If marketing managers are to take a long-term profitability viewpoint, they should consider predicating part of their compensation bonus on the long-term profitability of the product rather than on the product's profitability only when the manager is formally associated with the product. An accrual account could be built into the bonus system based on long-term performance of the product or service with which the managers are associated.

The technology for decision support in computing, models of consumer behavior, and market response models is way ahead of the impact of these advancements on the profitability of firms. It is top management's actions in the kind of people they hire and the motivations that are given to those people to balance the long- and short-term costs and profits that will unleash this technology to its true potential. Until top managers take a much more aggressive posture toward improving the decision support for their advertising and promotion decisions, the technology's potential will be much larger than its actual impact on firm profitability.

Summary and Action Questions

- Is decision support a fitting last substantive chapter to this book? What other areas do you feel are more important that you need help in?
- Go through the marketing information routinely used by the firm for advertising and promotion decision making. How much is market status information? How valuable is it for decision making? How much is market response information? How valuable is it for decision making?
- Does the firm have a decision support system for advertising and promotion? If not, why not? If a DSS is in place, how effective are each of the parts (i.e., data, models, statistics, reporting, computer systems) considering the comments made in this chapter?
- Who are the firm's interface people? Are they positioned effectively to interface between the managers, the market, and the DSS?
- How are those involved with the firm's DSS recruited and rewarded? Do these actions create incentives so that the advertising and promotion decisions are consistant with the firm's long-term overall strategic objectives?

176   *The Advertising and Promotion Challenge*

Further Readings

J. D. C. Little, "Decision Support for Marketing Management," *Journal of Marketing* (Summer 1979), pp. 9–26. A management overview of all the issues involved in evaluating, designing, and successfully implementing decision support systems in marketing.

M. Ibrahim, and L. M. Lodish, "Toward an Expert Decision Support System for Trade Promotions," Working Paper (The Marketing Department, The Wharton School, University of Pennsylvania, 1984). A decision support system for planning and evaluating trade promotions that incorporates aspects of artificial intelligence.

L. M. Lodish, and D. R. Riebstein, "Goldmines or Minefields for Marketing Research," *Howard Business Review*, to appear January/February 1986. A catalogue of the benefits and potential dangers of the new data and technologies to help marketing decision makers.

Notes

1. M. Ibrahim, and L. M. Lodish, "Toward an Expert Decision Support System for Trade Promotions," Working Paper (The Marketing Department, The Wharton School, University of Pennsylvania, 1984).
2. R. J. Schreiber, C. S. Schiller, and M. Bilkin, "The Effects of Frequency in Magazines and Purchasing Behavior," Presentation to the Advertising Research Foundation (New York, N.Y., June 1982).
3. "The Metric Coupon Laboratory," Brochure (Waltham, Massachusetts: Management Decision Systems, Inc., 1982).
4. *Ibid.*

◆ 11 ◆

Concluding Questions

In order to summarize the main points of this book, two sets of action questions are included: one for top management and the other for marketing management (including advertising and promotion management). Each question is followed by a notation of the chapter(s) in which it is discussed. Chief executive officers should not only be concerned with the set of questions for top management. They must also make sure that the questions for marketing managers are also being addressed. There is a big opportunity for improving advertising and promotion decisions and CEOs can take advantage of this opportunity by taking steps to satisfactorily answer these questions.

Top Management Questions

- Has the learning curve been applicable to the organization's marketing, advertising, and promotion expenditures? (Chapter 1)
- Are long-term organizational learning objectives in the key managers' management by objectives (MBO's)? (Chapters 1 and 10)
- Have all the possible roles been evaluated for advertising and promotion for the firm's products and services? (Chapters 2 and 3)
- Is the firm's corporate and product positioning strategy consis-

tent with the firm's advertising and promotion? (Chapters 2, 3, and 4)

- Has the resource allocation to advertising, promotion, and other marketing mix elements been considered as part of the corporate and marketing strategy? (Chapter 4)
- Are the firm's advertising and promotion objectives related to the firm's profitability? (Chapter 5)
- Has implementation of long-term programs to get more valuable information for advertising and promotion budgeting been encouraged? (Chapters 6 and 10)
- Has marketing management been encouraged to take appropriate steps to improve the profitability of the firm's advertising and promotion copy? (Chapter 7)
- Does the same person who sets the advertising or promotion budget also set the advertising or promotion testing budget? (Chapters 6 and 10)
- Are incentives in place both within the organization itself and with outside suppliers so that the firm is making more vaguely right decisions on media planning? (Chapter 8 and 9)
- Is a periodic audit requested for how well the firm's structure for obtaining advertising and promotion decisions is working? (Chapter 9)
- Do reports from marketing management include market response elements as well as market status elements? (Chapter 10)
- Does marketing management have suitable control and resources for development of marketing decision support systems? (Chapter 10)
- Is the development of interface people within the organization encouraged and rewarded? (Chapter 10)

Marketing Management Questions

- Can the roles for advertising and promotion be translated into operational objectives? (Chapters 2, 3, and 5)
- Are all of the firm's advertising and promotion roles consistent with long- or short-term profitability increases? (Chapters 2 and 3)
- How specifically does the firm's advertising and promotion relate to consumer's perception and preferences compared to competition? (Chapters 2 and 3)
- Does the consumer perceive any difference between the firm's promotions and price changes? (Chapter 3)

- Is the role of trade advertising and trade promotion consistent with the consumer advertising and promotion? (Chapters 2 and 3)
- Which operational, measurable advertising and promotion objectives may be precisely wrong? (Chapter 5)
- Is the firm managing the uncertainty in advertising and promotion budgeting or running away from it? (Chapter 6)
- Have continuous advertising and promotion testing programs been instituted? (Chapters 6 and 10)
- When the product, distribution, or pricing are changed, is the advertising or promotion budget adjusted appropriately? (Chapter 6)
- Does the organization, remuneration, and motivation of the firm's advertising and promotion suppliers encourage rational, unbiased, profitable answers to the copy, media, and budget questions for advertising and promotion? (Chapters 6, 7, 8, 9, and 10)
- Is the validity and reliability of the copy tests being used by the firm known? (Chapter 7)
- Are steps being taken to maximize the variabilities of copy alternatives that are evaluated by the firm's copy tests? (Chapter7)
- Are vaguely right decisions on media planning being supported with appropriate research, testing, and experimentation? (Chapters 8 and 10)
- Does the firm's advertising and promotion service structure maximize its advantages and minimize its disadvantages? (Chapter 8)
- Is the compensation method for outside suppliers consistent with maximizing their contribution to the firm's profitability? (Chapter 9)
- Is the firm's marketing decision support system structured so it has maximal value to the organization? (Chapter 10)
- Are the ways that decision support systems can be misused being countered by appropriate use of interface people? (Chapter 10)

Glossary

Advertising Nonpersonal forms of communication conducted through paid media under clear sponsorship.

Advertising roles Possible uses for advertising as part of the marketing mix.

Advertising tonnage The total potential exposures from an advertising schedule.

Affordable budgeting Budgeting up to what an entity can afford.

Audience of schedule The people potentially exposed to a media schedule; counted by a rating service.

Category positioning Trying to be perceived as part of a category (e.g., luxury cars).

Collateral house A firm specializing in advertising support services.

Competitive parity budgeting Budgeting to be similar to your competition.

Consumer advertising Advertising to the end user of a product or service.

Convergent validity Two independent answers to the same question that imply the same action.

Copy test reliability How likely it is to get similar answers if the same test is run.

Copy test validity Is the test measuring what it's supposed to be measuring (i.e., the sales effect of the advertising)?

Corporate advertising Advertising about a corporation rather than its products.

181

Creative boutique
An independent firm providing creative services—copy and art—to advertisers.

Dealing
Temporary price reductions or other short-term promotions.

Decision support system (DSS)
A coordinated system of data, statistics, models, computers, reporting, and graphics to aid in decision making.

Econometric research
Developing and estimating mathematical relationships that describe a system.

Efficiency effect
Achieved when advertising does the same job, but more efficiently, by reaching more people or getting more people to pay attention.

Equilibrium share
Point at which market share will level out after a disturbance (e.g., a new product introduction).

Equilibrium sales
Point at which sales will level out after a disturbance.

Evoking
Considering a brand or product as possible to purchase or definitely not to purchase.

Experience curve (learning curve)
The concept that costs per unit of production decrease as more units are produced.

Frequency
The average number of times an average person reached by a media schedule is potentially exposed to the schedule.

Gresham's law
Bad money drives out good money.

Gross rating points (GRPs)
The total number of potential exposures to a population divided by the number of people times 100 (i.e., 200 GRPs is the equivalent of 2 exposures to each person in the population).

Instrumented test markets
Markets where split cable TV and scanner panels are used to unobtrusively monitor advertising, promotion, and their sales affects at a household level.

Interface people
People who are the liaison between decision support systems and management.

Intermediary advertising
Advertising to channel members, like wholesalers, who are not the end user.

Learning curve (experience curve)
See *Experience curve.*

Marketing mix
All of the marketing variables: price, product, positioning, advertising, promotion, channels of distribution, and salesforce.

Matrix approach to market strategy	Classifying product/markets by two dimensions such as growth and market share and using this as a basis for strategic decisions on resource allocation.
Media audience	The people counted by rating services as being in the audience of a particular TV show or magazine, etc.
Naturally occurring experiments	Situations where different levels of marketing variables were used and may be evaluated to see which worked better.
Niche strategies	Aiming a product or service at a specialized market segment.
Objective budgeting	Budgeting to achieve some objective (e.g., reaching at least 70% of the population an average of 3 times).
Percentage of sales budgeting	Budgeting advertising and promotion at a fixed percentage of sales.
Perceptual change	Changing people's perception or image of a product or service.
Potential exposures	People counted by rating services as exposed to a media vehicle or TV show or magazine. This does not mean that all the people will be exposed to your particular ad, however.
Product positioning	The process of trying to improve the perception of your product by a market segment.
Promotion	Short-term incentives designed to stimulate earlier or stronger market response.
Rating point	1% of a population counted as being potentially exposed to a media vehicle.
Reach	The percentage of a population potentially exposed to an ad campaign at least once.
Reliable copy testing	See *Copy test reliability*.
Scale effect	Multiplying the response to advertising by a constant factor.
Scanner panel	A group of people who carry a card that records all of their purchases at food and drug stores via UPC scanners.
Simulated laboratories	Laboratory situations that simulate real marketing situations, such as new product introductions.
Speculative presentations	Presentation work by advertising agencies to try to get new accounts.

Split Cable TV   Cable TV systems where cut-ins can be made so at the same time different cable subscribers tuned to the same channel will get different advertisements.

Split run   Putting different ads in every other edition of a newspaper or magazine.

Task budgeting   Budgeting enough money to achieve a specific task—such as getting 90% awareness.

Trade advertising   See *Intermediary advertising*.

Trade-off   Evaluating two alternatives compared to each other.

Trade promotion   Promotion to the trade or intermediaries, not to the final consumer.

Unduplicated audience   The same as the reach of a schedule—see *Reach*.

Valid copy testing See *Copy test*.

What/if scenario   Predicting *what* would happen *if* certain actions are taken.

Index